FROM THE PRAIRIES TO PERU—AND BEYOND

A GIFT OF APPRECIATION
FROM
ABWE PLANNED GIVING
MINISTRIES

FROM THE PRAIRIES TO PERU—AND BEYOND

A Canadian Family's Adventure Along the Amazon

IVOR AND RUTH GREENSLADE

Association of Baptists for World Evangelism
P.O. Box 8585
Harrisburg, PA 17105-8585
(717) 774-7000
E-mail: abwe@abwe.org

ABWE Canada
160 Adelaide St. South, Suite 205
London, Ontario N5Z 3L1
(519) 690-1009
E-mail: office@abwecanada.org

 PUBLISHING®

FROM THE PRAIRIES TO PERU—AND BEYOND
A Canadian Family's Adventure Along the Amazon
Copyright © 2002 by ABWE Publishing
Harrisburg, Pennsylvania 17105

Library of Congress Cataloging-in Publications Data (application pending)

Greenslade, Ivor, 1926–
Greenslade, Ruth Phillips, 1928–
    From the Prairies to Peru—and Beyond
    Missions, Non-fiction
    ISBN: 1-888796-30-8

Printed in the United States of America.

TABLE OF CONTENTS

DEDICATION

This book is lovingly dedicated to our children:

Tom

David

Kathy

Betty

Karen

Cindy

In gratefulness to God for the
great family He gave us.

ACKNOWLEDGMENTS

The idea of this book started with the people at Central Baptist Church, Brantford, Ontario, who, upon hearing our many stories, kept saying, "You should write a book." Thank you for planting the seed and encouraging us to keep going to the end.

Writing *From the Prairies to Peru—and Beyond* brought back a flood of memories of God's work in our lives and in the people it was our privilege to touch in our ministries.

This book would not have been possible without the letters Dorothy Penrice, Betty and Dave Ganton, Ruth's mother, and our children kept all these years. When they heard we were thinking of writing this account, they passed them all to us, canceling the excuse that we didn't have enough material. Thank you for doing this.

Knowing Ruth's ability to write interesting prayer letters and articles for the ABWE *Message* magazine, we decided to share in this book. We are thankful to God for bringing us together.

Special thanks to the faculty and students of the London Bible Institute (now Tyndale College), who influenced our lives and guided us through the first steps to missionary work.

We are also grateful to God for our colleagues on the ABWE Upper Amazon Field Council in Peru, the Argentine Field Council in Buenos Aires, and the national pastors and leaders in both of these countries. We express our sincerest thanks to all of them.

We thank our publisher, the Association of Baptists for World Evangelism (ABWE), under whose auspices we have served since 1954. And a special thank-you goes to Jeannie Lockerbie Stephenson, our editor. Her writing tips, talent, creativity, suggestions, corrections, and deadline-setting kept us moving ahead to final completion.

Thank you to Don and Grace Perkins for opening their retreat center, Shepherd's Care, so we could get away for a few days at a time to better concentrate on the task.

A special thank-you to our pastor, Dr. Brent Powell, and the deacons at Central Baptist Church Brantford, for time off from associate pastor duties and the encouragement to "get that book done."

Our missionary life would not have been possible without our supporters, both churches and individuals, who sponsored us in our ministry and prayed for us. We express a deep and sincere "thank you" to all of them.

Ivor and Ruth Greenslade
May 2002

FOREWORD

Mark Twain said on one occasion, "Moon talk by those who have never been on the moon is rather dull whereas war talk by those who have been to war is most exciting." *From the Prairies to Peru—and Beyond* is not moon talk but war talk by those who have been on the front lines of battle and have witnessed many victories as they have submitted to the orders of their commanding officer, the Lord of the Harvest.

With the changing face of missions, much of what is being written has to do with the trends and theory of missions today. This helps to keep us up to date on what is happening in our world and shows how we can adapt our methodology to fulfill the Great Commission. But it is refreshing to read Ivor and Ruth's book, which comes from the heart and pen of mission practitioners, not theorists.

Anyone who reads this book with real application of heart and mind to its content will find that he cannot remain indifferent to the great task of proclaiming the gospel.

I have known Ivor and Ruth for over fifty years, and have followed their mission pilgrimage with great interest and thanksgiving. I have prayed for them throughout the long season of their dedication to the Lord.

In this book we see four contributors to Ivor and Ruth's greatness as missionary pioneers:

First, Ivor and Ruth love Jesus. Please don't think this is a mere saccharine appraisal among friends. Their love for Christ carries a subtle and pervasive authority that makes them believable. When you read them, you walk away from the experience knowing that what you've heard is the truth—the life-changing truth.

Second, Ivor and Ruth practice servant leadership. They teach others what they have learned in the laboratory of their own experience.

Third, Ivor and Ruth know the excitement of the love of God spreading out to a lost world. They understand the tremendous battle taking place between the forces of light and darkness.

Finally, they are good communicators. It is not often that good oral communicators are good with the pen. But throughout this book, you will find the paragraphs coming and going so smoothly that you can't put it down until you have finished the last chapter.

As you read this book, you will experience the passion in your heart, melting the lead in your feet and the ice on your tongues, and driving you to full obedience. You will recognize the truth of the saying, "only one life, twill soon be past; only what's done for Christ will last."

Dr. Roy Lawson
Former Secretary of the Fellowship of
  Evangelical Baptist Churches in Canada
June 2002

CHAPTER ONE

Early Days on the Prairie

"Why, you little toad!" the nurse exclaimed after my mother's
frantic call on July 14, 1926.

I was born 20 minutes after my sister, Irene, in the Hanna
Hospital, in Alberta, the ninth of eleven children. Dr. W. W.
Cross delivered my twin sister, but they didn't know about
me. I came along after they took my mother back to her room.
With no doctor or nurse on hand, and the call bell not working,
Mom had to pound on the hot water register with a bedpan to
get someone's attention. "Toad" became my nickname, and it
stuck for years. My brothers said I looked like a toad because my
nose spread across my face.

My father, William Henry Greenslade, emigrated to Canada
from Bristol, England, in 1902 and joined the Canadian Pacific
Railway in Winnipeg, Manitoba. Later he homesteaded eight
miles east of Nanton, Alberta, south of Calgary, staying there for
six years. In the winters he worked as a carpenter at the Banff
Springs Hotel, or in the bush, snaking out logs. His brother,
Walter Frances, joined him later.

In 1909, the Greenslade brothers bought supplies at Bassano,
east of Calgary, and headed northeast across open prairie, arriving at the easternmost bend of Berry Creek. Dad chose this spot
because he knew of the plans to build a railroad across the
prairies to Calgary. The railroad was to cross the Berry Creek at
that very spot. Dad said, "Where there's water and a railroad,

there will be a town." Dad and Uncle Walt built a one-room shack and a small barn. The closest neighbors were 30 miles to the west; to the north and east lay nothing but open prairie. By 1913 most of the area was settled on the quarter sections (160 acre plots) the government allotted. During the next 10 years, most of those homesteaders left. That area of Alberta doesn't have enough rain to support a dense population.

Mother came from Yatton, in Somerset County, England, in 1912, and settled with her mother and stepfather two miles west of the Berry Creek. Mother and Dad were married in 1914. Their first child, Dorothy, born in 1915, died in infancy. I never knew about her until September of 1939, when my 17-year-old brother, Bill, was killed on the farm. Dad declared he would not bottle up Bill's death as he had Dorothy's. Dad said Dorothy's death was as fresh in his mind as the day it happened.

My earliest memories are of my twin sister, Irene. We played together and got into trouble together. When we were about three years old, we slipped away from the house and headed through the barnyard, past the poplar trees to beyond the farm buildings. We wanted to watch Dad and Uncle Walt seeding a field. When Uncle Walt's team of six horses saw us, they spooked and ran away, smashing a brand new drill on a pile of rocks. I can still see one of the horses rearing up and the whole team tearing off with my uncle pulling on the lines—without effect. I also remember Dad's anger when he came into the house and told my mother to keep my sister and me in (or at least near) the house.

Our mother said Irene and I didn't speak English at first. We had our own language, part of which included spitting. Apparently, Irene and I had no trouble understanding each other.

We didn't have store-bought toys so we made our own. Irene and I ran with long sticks in each hand as if they were another pair of legs. The sticks were our horses and we named them after the real horses on the farm. We also were fond of marking up books with pencils or crayons, and sometimes cutting them with scissors. If we got caught, Irene would say, "It was Iowa" (her name for me). Once when she was spanked for cutting pages in a book, I stood back laughing in delight. She had finally gotten caught in the act and couldn't blame me. My delight quickly faded when I was spanked for laughing at her.

Until we were nine years old, Irene was bigger than I was, and could run faster. It was a great day for me when I passed her and won a race for the first time. Irene also started riding horses before I did. When I was placed on a horse, I felt as if I were on a high cliff; I was terrified. I was five years old when my brothers first got me on old Jim. Someone slapped him on the rump and he set out at a full gallop. Since I was riding bareback, I hung onto Jim's mane with all my might. The reins lay on his neck, but no way was I going to let go of my only security to catch them. Staying on his back consumed my entire attention. I didn't know anything about steering. All went well until Jim turned a corner. He turned, but I kept going straight, tumbling to the ground. Old Jim stopped and looked at me. I got up uninjured, led him to a barbed wire fence, climbed a post using the wires as steps, and got back on Jim. I was determined I wasn't going to be called a "scaredy cat." After that episode, my brothers taught me to ride properly.

During the summer months, we kids went riding every Sunday afternoon. There was only one saddle, which the oldest generally claimed. The rest of us rode bareback. We headed out across the sparsely populated prairies to visit the five bachelors who lived within reasonable riding distance from home.

In homesteading days, there was a shortage of women on the prairies, and some men had no source for a bride. Uncle Walt, for example, didn't marry until he was 75. A couple of the bachelors were rather strange, and others were shy; I don't think they would have married even if there had been women available. Two of them lived in one-room shacks. Two lived in small houses.

People on the prairies never locked their doors, even when

they were not at home. There was an unwritten rule that all homes should be accessible to a traveler in need. It was also understood that if the traveler was hungry, he could help himself to whatever food was in the house. The bachelors always went away on Sundays. So when we Greenslade children arrived at their homes, we felt free to help ourselves if we were hungry, and even when we weren't.

We thought none of the men would know who visited their places. This dream was crushed when a couple of my brothers met one of the bachelors on the road one day. He told them, "I don't mind you eating the bread, and I don't mind you eating the jam, but please close the door when you leave so the flies won't get in." We had been found out!

I started grade one at Sunny Valley School, located in the basement of the Plymouth Brethren Hall. The school had been moved from the old McKellar house, which was too small for the growing student body.

Early in the fall of 1933, my family moved six miles (9 km) west so my older brothers could attend high school in Rose Lynn, the closest town to our home on the Berry Creek.

I liked my teacher at Sunny Valley School, but detested the one at Rose Lynn whose discipline was physical and drastic. Happily, in the spring, Dad and Mom, with the younger family members, moved back to Berry Creek, where I attended Sunny Valley School through grade 10. One teacher taught all the grades in that one-room school. We received an education equal—if not superior—to that given in the larger, multiple-room schools in the province. The younger ones often hurried to get their work done so they could listen to what the older grades were being taught, and the older students often helped the younger pupils.

School started at 9:00 a.m. Our daily assignments were written on the blackboard, so as soon as classes started we set to work while the teacher moved from grade to grade. We enjoyed a short recess both in the morning and afternoon, with a one-hour break for lunch. In the warm months, we ate outside. During winter, we ate at our desks, then went outside to play. The main winter sports were "fox and geese," and snow battles between the forts we built. In the summer we played softball and prisoners base.

The school population fluctuated between 15 and 25 students. My family lived a little over three miles (5 km) away. In the summer we went by horse and buggy, or a team and "democrat"—a longer form of the buggy. In the winter we traveled by team and sleigh, as long as feed for the horses held out. When there was a shortage of feed, we had to walk. In those days, snow on the level prairie piled up anywhere from two to three feet deep, which meant walking wasn't easy. And with the temperature standing at 30°F (35°C) *below zero,* it was even worse. I remember one week of 55°F *below zero* when we still went to school by team and sleigh, but the horses refused to trot, even though we tried to make them do so. The cold air would have frozen their lungs. The horses had more sense than we did. In the oven of our coal-burning stove, we heated big rocks that we placed in straw on the bottom of the sleigh. We put our feet against them and covered ourselves with quilts. When we got to school, we students sat in a circle around the big furnace. Our fronts were warm, but our backs were cold, so we had to turn around once in a while to get warm all over.

All the school children were interested in earning money. We did so by catching gophers and raiding crows' nests. We received one cent for each gopher tail and crows' egg, but five whole cents for a pair of crows' legs. This was a government program set up as an attempt to cut down the pest population of the province.

My favorite way to catch gophers was with a snare made from twine. I looped twine around the gopher's hole; then I stood back holding the three-foot-long string. I waited for the gopher to poke its head out, then yanked on the string, tightening the loop around its neck. I thumped it on the ground, which meant a rapid death for the gopher. If it delayed in poking its head up, I patted the ground just outside the hole with the palm of my hand. The gopher almost always stuck its head up to see what was going on.

It was necessary to climb trees to get the crows' eggs and the legs of the young crows in the nest. We pricked a hole in each end of the egg, blew out the contents, and carefully packed the shells in grass for transportation to the school. Broken shells were not acceptable. To get the young crows' legs, we had to kill them and cut off their legs.

We didn't have any other way of making money as we grew up during the Depression, when the entire country was in an economic crunch. We were not paid for doing chores, as everyone in the family was expected to pitch in and help make ends meet. It was a great day when we were given a penny or five cents to buy candy at the store, a rare occurrence. We rarely had jam on our table, but we always had large cans of corn syrup. These cans, when empty, were turned into lunch pails. If I had written a story about my school days, I could have used the title "Syrup Pails and Gopher Tails."

My family was not religious. We received little Bible teaching other than that given by the teachers at school. My dad was raised in a strict Anglican background, and claimed he was obligated to learn about religion. He decided when he turned 16, he wanted nothing more to do with it. He claimed he couldn't believe in a God who would create hell in which to punish people forever. He did, however, know many facts about the Bible. During mealtimes, we often had heated discussions. To settle a point, Dad would say, "Get down the Bible." When we handed it to him, he would say, "This is the Book of Books of the Lord of Lords." I learned to hold a high respect for the Bible, but didn't learn its contents.

When Irene and I were five, our mother sent us on an errand to the Burkinshaw house, a little more than a mile (1.6 km) from our home. Mrs. Burkinshaw asked, "Would you like to see Grandfather and Grandmother?" We didn't know what she was talking about because we had never heard those words before, but we were curious. "Yes," we dutifully replied. Mrs. Burkinshaw took us into the living room. Sitting beside a table was a woman with a wrinkled face and a man with a long, white pointed beard. He talked to us in a high voice using words not allowed in our home, as they were classed as swear words. When we arrived home, I asked my mother why he could use those words and we couldn't. She told me, "He was probably preaching the gospel." I didn't know what she meant.

In Sunny Valley School, sometimes the teacher directed individual students or groups of students to sing for the other pupils. One day, two students sang a duet that sounded to me like, "All the way to *Calgary* he went for me." I wondered who had gone to Calgary and why. I knew nothing of Calvary, the hill on which Jesus was crucified.

CHAPTER TWO

From a Soldier in the Canadian Army to a Soldier of the King

The Second World War started while I was in Sunny Valley School. My oldest brother joined the English RAF (Royal Air Force) in 1933, became a pilot, and flew bombers over Europe. He was killed when his plane was shot down over Holland, on October 2, 1942. Four other brothers joined the armed services. My father recommended I leave school and join the army, so that after the war I would have government help to pay for my education. I was soon to be conscripted into the army anyway, so I joined the Canadian Army on October 4, 1944. I took two months of basic training at Wetaskiwin, Alberta; two months of advanced training at Petewawa, Ontario; and two months of battle training at Vernon, British Columbia—preparing for action as part of the Sixth Canadian Division heading to the Pacific to invade Japan. The war in the Pacific ended the day we were to board the train to Seattle, en route to Guam, so I did not see active duty.

After the end of World War II, I was transferred to Ottawa, Ontario, to serve in the Headquarters Office of the Canadian Army Service Corp. A friend guided me into contact with Christian military personnel who invited me to attend Metropolitan Bible Church and a Bible study held by the SACA (Soldiers and Airmen's Christian Association), led by Major Gymenat. Through that church and those Bible studies, I came to know Christ as my Savior in February 1946.

This changed the whole direction of my life. A few weeks after my salvation in a youth meeting where Chuck Templeton was the speaker, I came to the firm conviction that I was called by God to preach the gospel. I told Major Gymenat and asked him what I should do. He said, "You need to go to a Bible institute to prepare for the ministry." I had never heard of a Bible institute and asked, "Where do I find one?" He recommended London Bible Institute (LBI) in London, Ontario. I asked for my discharge from the army—leaving one army and marching into another.

I had been saved only eight months when I entered LBI in September 1946. With my non-religious background, I had many things to learn—and unlearn. I am grateful for the patience of the faculty in guiding me into Christian maturity. I am also thankful for the help I received from fellow students who had many more years of experience in serving God.

In the months after my conversion, I attended Metropolitan Bible Church in Ottawa. I would arrive about 15 minutes early for the Sunday morning service. A few minutes later, people poured in through the doors of the auditorium. I wondered how so many people could arrive at the same time on the city's public transportation. I didn't know they were coming from the Sunday school held before the 11:00 a.m. service. I was never told about the classes, nor invited to attend. My first time in Sunday school was as a teacher.

On a Friday, one week after entering LBI, a student in my apartment rushed up to me saying, "I need to go home urgently to help my mother." He slapped what I thought was a small magazine in my hand and said, "This is the Sunday school manual. I need someone to teach my class." Then he ran out to catch a bus. He had written the address of where the Sunday school was held and the lesson for that week. I turned to another classmate, Bern Flannagan, and asked, "Bern, what's a Sunday school?" Bern laughed, but then sat down to show me what to do. I prepared according to his directions and went on Sunday morning to the indicated location. I could hear the noise from the children before I saw the building. My job was to teach 20 boys, ages 12 to 14. I don't remember anything about that class. It must have been a bad experience. But that showed me I needed to attend Sunday school and learn more of the Bible.

At LBI they gave an entrance exam of 100 questions to all the incoming students to test their Bible knowledge for placement in classes. I answered only three of the questions, and got all three wrong because of my lack of biblical knowledge. The registrar placed me in what was called the "Prep year," where the basics of the Bible and theology were taught. This meant I needed to take an extra year, but it was necessary for me.

I persevered at LBI for six years and graduated with a bachelor of theology degree in May 1952, from what was then named London Bible College and Theological Seminary, now Tyndale College. At Bible college, I met a fellow student named Ruth Phillips.

Ruth tells her story:

> I was born in the fishing town of Port Dover, Ontario, 30 miles (48 km) south of Brantford on Lake Erie. My father, Harry Edward, was a commercial fisherman. I am the eldest of five children. The other four are Bill, Bob, Mary Ann, and Susan. I am almost 20 years older than my youngest sister and was preparing for Bible school when she was born. My brother, Bill, has been a missionary in French Canada as long as I have been in South America. During his last year of seminary, he, along with other seminary students and pastors, went to Quebec to minister on weekends. He and several others were put in jail for three months for preaching in an open-air meeting.
>
> When I was four, my family moved to Brantford. One year later, my dad was injured on his job and was unable to work, so had to go on welfare. His pride was hurt and he always said he was going to pay the welfare back. Then my

brother Bill contracted polio. The doctor said Bill would probably not live, but if he did, he would never walk. This was more
than Dad could take. We moved into a house across from the
Missionary Alliance Tabernacle. The people there invited my
parents to church. Dad used to say, "I told them I went to
church to be christened and married, and I don't expect to go
again until I die." But his pride was broken by his sickness, the
Depression fall-out, loss of his job, and Bill's polio, so he and
Mom began attending church. Shortly afterward, Dad was
saved.

My brother, Bill, says his suffering all these years is worth
it just to have Dad become a Christian. If Dad had not been
saved, our lives would have been different. Following treatment, Bill was able to walk again. Despite some limitations
from the polio, Bill has led an active life, and, with his wife,
Blanche, serves God in Quebec.

My brother, Bob, was assistant coach to Wayne Gretzky,
one of Canada's greatest hockey players. It was Bob who
taught Wayne to go in behind the net and tuck the puck in for
a goal.

My father never stayed in one house long. Every three
years or so, he would buy a house, fix it up, and sell it. God was
preparing me for frequent moves at an early age. I never got
settled down and used to one area or one set of friends. I
attended four different schools from kindergarten to grade
eight. In missionary life, I lived in 33 different houses; moving
from one place to another never bothered me.

I attended Central Baptist Church, in Brantford, with my
parents in the morning, and Rawdon Street Mission in the
afternoon. At this mission, at the age of 10, I accepted the Lord
as my personal Savior. I was very shy and did not like the fact
that I had red hair and was covered with freckles. The women
at church thought my hair was beautiful, but the children at
school often recited an unflattering poem about redheads.

I was baptized at the age of 12 at Central Baptist Church.
For several years my family attended Muskoka Baptist Camp

in Huntsville, Ontario. It was there, during my high school years, under the teaching of Rev. DeLoss Scott, I dedicated my life to the Lord for whatever He wanted me to do

I attended Brantford Collegiate Institute, finishing grade 10. At 16 years of age, I was old enough to go to work. Because I was the eldest, it was decided I should work to help the family. I worked with other women as a "number please" girl at Bell Telephone. I sat on a high stool wearing earphones. When a light shone on the board, I placed a plug into the hole that was illuminated and said, "Number, please." The caller gave the number he or she wanted, then I took another plug and inserted it into the hole of the requested number and rang that phone. I was on duty the night World War II ended. All the lights went on at once. Everyone was calling to see why the factory whistles were blowing. All of us on duty hopped off our stools and moved up and down the bank of lights, plugging our cords into one hole after another, saying, "The war is over." Slowly the lights went off, till we were able to get back to a normal call load.

When I had saved enough money, I attended Day's Business College, in Brantford, for six months, learning typing and shorthand. After graduating, I got a job as secretary in one of the Cockshutt Plough offices, earning $100 a month. After working there for two years, I became unsettled and discontented. I couldn't understand what was happening because I loved my job. Then I remembered my promise to God: I would do whatever He wanted me to. I handed in my resignation and started attending London Bible Institute in September 1947. Because of not having a high school diploma, I had to take a preparatory class, making my course last four years rather than three. It was there I met Ivor and, after my graduation, we were married on June 28, 1952. Our first son, Thomas Edward, was born on June 17, 1953.

God knew I needed a wife who was raised in a Christian home. We have worked as a close team for all the years of our ministries. I'm grateful to God for bringing us together.

In November 1952, Clarence Jones from radio station HCJB (Heralding Christ Jesus' Blessings), "The Voice of the Andes" in Quito, Ecuador, was the missionary speaker at Central Baptist Church, Brantford. He challenged the congregation for missionary work in both the Sunday services at Central, and later in the evening at a Youth for Christ rally at the Capital Theater. In each service I sensed a growing urge to respond to that challenge. On the way to our car after the youth rally, I asked Ruth, "Are we to serve in South America?" She answered, "Yes." We went back into the theater to talk with Clarence Jones. I told him we had come to the firm conviction we were to serve as missionaries in South America. He asked brusquely, "How's your health?" I told him doctors thought I might have a problem with my heart. He said, "Forget it. You need a strong body to fight the battles against the devil." Then he turned and walked away.

His response made us pause, but we made missionary work a matter of prayer. At that time, I worked as a bulldozer operator at the Ontario hydroelectric construction project at Niagara Falls, commuting each week from Brantford in a 1932 Ford. One Monday morning in December, I was a bit late for work, so I pushed the old car faster than was wise. Suddenly I heard a thundering knock in the motor—a main bearing had burned out. I knew fellow LBI students Mel and Dorothy Cuthbert lived a short distance off the highway near where the car trouble started. Mel's mother's house was near the highway, so I left the car in her yard and walked a short distance to Mel's house to explain why my car was there.

During my half hour with the Cuthberts, Mel asked me what Ruth and I planned to do with our lives. I told him of our missionary call. He told me he and Dorothy had recently been accepted by the Association of Baptists for World Evangelism (ABWE), and spoke of that mission in glowing terms. I left their house with the conviction Ruth and I should join the same mission.

We applied to ABWE, and were invited to attend the

month-long candidate classes held in March 1954. Nine-month-old Tom stayed with Grandma and Grandpa Phillips. We arrived knowing the Lord wanted us to work in South America, but we didn't know exactly where and needed the Lord's guidance. After a couple of weeks, we stood with others of the 13 candidates in front of a world map at the mission house in Germantown, Pennsylvania. Candidate secretary Bob Burns walked up, slapped his finger on that map, and said, "That field hasn't had new missionaries for years." He took his finger off and walked away. Right under his finger was a place called Nauta, in Peru. Ruth and I, at that moment, felt the leading of the Lord to Nauta. We didn't know it at that time, but Nauta was where Bill and Ruth Large, other Canadian missionaries we knew, were stationed. At the end of candidate classes, we met with the ABWE board and were assigned to Upper Amazon, Peru.

After picking up Tom in Brantford, we spent the summer months of 1954 at MBC (Muskoka Baptist Conference). Ruth taught the children's classes and I was a general flunky, a handyman who fixed a lot of things.

After our time at MBC, Ruth and I started deputation (now called Pre-field Ministries). We began visiting churches, looking for sponsors to support us. These trips led us to several Canadian provinces as well as the United States.

The first individuals who promised us support were Dr. Bill and Maureen Foster. He taught at Baptist Bible College in Johnson City, New York, then at the London College of Bible and Missions, in London, Ontario, and later at Ontario Theological Seminary in Toronto, Ontario.

Our son David arrived before we expected him. At 3:00 a.m., February 9, 1955, things began happening fast. I was afraid our baby would be born in the car, so I called the fire department for an ambulance. There was a big fire in Brantford that night. The lone fireman left at the fire hall had to wait until a policeman arrived to accompany him to our house. They finally came and took Ruth to the hospital. David was born shortly after she was admitted. That evening's *Brantford Expositor* ran a full article on the fire and the resulting lack of firemen to run the ambulance and take a woman in labor to the hospital.

Through the fall of 1954 and all of 1955, we visited many churches. During the summer of 1955, we went to Alberta to visit Grandpa Greenslade and others in my family. David was just four months old. We took the back seat out of the 1939 Ford and put in a bassinet. At night we pulled off to the side of the road. We didn't have money for motels. Ruth slept across the front seat, which was long enough for her. Tom and Dave slept in the back seat area. I slept outside, next to the car.

All of our support was promised by December 1955. On December 28, Ruth's father drove us to the Toronto Airport in a crowded car. Two-year-old Tom sat on my lap in those days before the required use of seat belts. I spotted a plane in the distance and asked, "Tom, do you see that plane taking off up ahead?" "Yes," he answered. I told him, "That's the kind of plane we are going on." After a bit Tom began patting me on the knee and said, "Dad, you can't go on that plane. You're too big!"

At the airport we found a large group of people from our supporting churches to see us off. We presented ourselves at the counter, checked our bags, and were ready to go. The folk gathered around, sang a hymn of farewell, and one of them prayed before we headed out to the plane. Ruth had never flown before, and this would be a long trip. We were heading to Costa Rica to learn Spanish. We flew first to New York City, and then made three more stops before arriving in Miami early in the morning after an all-night trip.

Our flight to Costa Rica was to depart in the afternoon, so we had a long wait ahead. We knew no one in Miami, so we decided to stay at the airport and watch people go by. I noticed a tall man enter the large waiting room. He looked over the more than 100 people, then came straight to us. He asked, "Are you

Mr. Greenslade?" I answered, "Yes. How did you pick us out from among all these people?" He said, "I knew you were going to be here, and I can spot missionaries a mile away." This was a surprise to me, as I didn't think we looked different from anyone else.

The man was Mr. Wagler, who helped missionaries in South America. He had a large house with guest rooms and invited us to spend the day there. What a delight to have a place where we could rest and be served a good meal! In Miami we saw our first palm trees and heard the fronds clattering against each other in the wind.

We flew out of Miami on a two-motored Convair plane for San José, Costa Rica, arriving on December 29, 1955. We were met by ABWE missionaries Elmer and Marjorie Cassidy, from Toronto, and classmates of ours at London Bible Institute, and by Ruth's Aunt Claudia. A Costa Rican and the widow of Ruth's late uncle, Gladstone Franklin, former missionary to Costa Rica, Aunt Claudia had visited our family in Brantford. What a welcome—assuring us we were in good hands for our year of Spanish language study.

CHAPTER THREE

Language School

Elmer and Marj Cassidy were our "Big Brother and Sister," assigned to welcome and help our family adapt to Costa Rica. At the airport, we crowded into a taxi with all our bags. Elmer and Marj had attended the School of Languages for several months so were already quite adept with the language. On the way into the city, Elmer said something to the taxi driver who stopped in front of a dilapidated shack beside the road. Elmer said, "Well, here it is! A place for you to live. It has a dirt floor, but don't worry. The maid sweeps it every day so it should be quite comfortable." In my mind, I was ready to accept anything that was preparation for missionary work. I said, "Okay, Elmer. Whatever you have for us." He laughed and said something to the driver, who drove on to an aqua blue house with large picture windows, surrounded by lawns and cement retaining walls. This was our first residence in Costa Rica, not the tumbledown shack of Elmer's joke.

Ruth and I rented household necessities from the School of Languages. This included furniture, appliances, linens, and whatever else was needed. The school was equipped to handle over 100 missionaries at a time, supplying them with all they required for their rented homes.

Ruth and I knew no Spanish, not even how to say yes or no. We had entered a new culture, with many new experiences before us—all of them interesting, some exciting, and a few difficult. Seeing the new sights and sounds around us was a great adventure. Elmer introduced me to the buses and the downtown market where we would buy our food every week. He took me around to the various stands in the market, introduced me to the vendors, and told them I would be buying from them.

My first shopping trip was fine because Elmer explained the different foods and did all the buying. From then on, I was on my own. I pointed to what I wanted, held up my fingers for how much, handed over the money, and hoped I was given the right change. After learning enough Spanish to know what was going on, I realized some of the people were overcharging me. I began buying at other stands, much to the delight of those receiving my business.

One day I wanted to buy fish. I asked the man for a kilo of fish (*pescado* in Spanish) but left out the essential "s" in that word. Instead I asked for a kilo of *pecado,* which means "sin." I guess he thought I had enough already and laughed. At the time, I didn't realize my mistake because the vendor weighed up a kilo of fish. We language students learned to laugh at our mistakes and go on.

Since Ruth needed to study Spanish full time as well as I, that meant we needed to hire a woman to baby-sit our children and prepare meals while we took classes during the morning and studied in the afternoon. The School of Languages advertised for housekeepers. Three women agreed to come for interviews. Each one named the day and time they would come. Not one showed up. Ruth and I were told the women didn't want to hurt our feelings so said they would come even though they had no intention of doing so. Those housekeepers spoke only Spanish. We spoke only English, which is probably why they were reluctant to work for us.

Then a woman who had never worked for North Americans appeared. She cleaned everything in sight, washing whatever she found lying around. Ruth spent a lot of time with her, showing her how to cook and do other things. The language school supplied us with a two-column word list which included the terms

Ruth, about ten years old, in front of her grandmother's house in Brantford

Ivor and his twin sister Irene, eleven years old, taken on the farm in Alberta

Our wedding in Brantford Ontario, on June 28, 1952

BI graduation in London, May 1951

Tom and Emilio Rengifo holding the boa that was under the tree in our yard

Our family in our backyard in Nautua by the palm tree where the snake was found

A floating gas station where we bought fuel

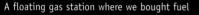

Traveling with our family and Steven Bond, son of Don and Vivian Bond, on the ABEM launch

The Greenslade family standing on the point where the Ucayali River (on the right) and the Marañón River (on the left) form the Amazon River

Ruth with the parrot that could say 300 words in English and Spanish and sing "Happy Birthday"

Typical houses along the Amazon and other rivers

A 6-foot Amazon fish called a *paiche*

Going for a baptismal service—the boat was filled to capacity with more people getting in. A favorite saying is, "Perhaps nothing will happen."

T.E.E. students arriving at the launch for their class

Emanuel Baptist
Church congregation
in front of Jesús and
Emma's house

Rev. Ricardo Panduro, pastor of
Emanuel Baptist Church, first
national director of Iquitos
Baptist Bible Institute

The portable
tabernacle we
built in sections
in our backyard
and erected on
the property of
Immanuel Baptist
Church

Ruth cooking on our
kerosene stove in
Iquitos

we needed to run the house. One column was in English, the other in Spanish. Ruth selected from the list what she wanted for meals or chores that needed to be done. She pointed them out on the list to no avail. That's when we discovered the housekeeper couldn't read. She let the boys do pretty much whatever they wanted. On arriving home one noon, we found 12-month-old David pushing his toy dump truck around on the floor, filled to the top with butter. The housekeeper thought it was funny. We didn't. That housekeeper didn't last long.

Through the language school, we were able to hire another woman. She seemed to be more comfortable with us. Then one day when Ruth and I were downtown shopping, we saw a woman sitting on the sidewalk, begging. She had a blood-soaked bandage wrapped around her leg, a common practice to gain the sympathy of potential donors. Something looked familiar about her. It was our housekeeper, on her day off, begging for money. She told us she could make more money there in one day than in working for us all week. Not long after the incident, she also quit, maybe to go into begging full time.

We were finally able to hire a Christian girl, Amelia, who had worked for several North American families. She could both read and write, and was cheerful, worked well with the children, and also was an excellent cook. Two-year-old Tom and one-year-old Dave cried as we left for classes for the first few days. But they quickly adjusted and learned Spanish faster than their parents.

Ruth and I felt like babes as we tried to learn the language step by step. The *Escuela de Idiomas* (the School of Languages) was set up specifically to teach Spanish to missionaries. All the teachers were from Costa Rica or other Latin American countries. In the school they were allowed to speak only Spanish. Rev. and Mrs. LaPorte, Presbyterians from the United States, directed the school. The teachers had become expert at bringing missionaries from no knowledge of Spanish to good fluency in one year's time.

The academic year was divided into three semesters. The year we arrived, about 130 missionaries representing 37 mission agencies attended the school. We had four classes each morning, plus chapel. Grammar was the only large class; all the others were divided into groups of three or four, to permit more personalized teaching. Classes for men and women were held separately.

I was placed with two other missionary men. The three of us were looking over our textbooks when our teacher arrived. We gaped for a moment at the beautiful woman who looked like a movie star. She sat down at our table, smiled, opened her book, and said something to us in Spanish. We didn't know what she said. She repeated it. We just looked at her. She pointed to page eight. We opened our books to the same page. She pointed to the first line, read it, and looked at me. I didn't know what I was supposed to do. She repeated the line, again looking at me. I just sat there. She repeated it again. Suddenly I understood I was to try to read the same words. She led me in doing this five times, then went on to the next man, repeating this in turn with each one of us. We didn't know what we were saying but the important thing was pronouncing the Spanish words. For example, we repeated again and again, *"La plancha está en la casa."* We didn't find out until later that we were saying, "The iron is in the house." Before we even knew the meaning of the words, we could say them correctly.

Another teacher arrived for the next hour, a class in phonetics. We found the secret of correct pronunciation of Spanish was to make sure we placed our tongues in the right position. In English, the tongue lazily floats around in the middle of the mouth. In Spanish, the tongue is moving all the time and must be placed in certain spots to produce the correct sounds. There is a different position for each of the vowels. For the "a" the tongue has to be at the front of the mouth. It moves back for each vowel until the "u," where the tongue has to be curled under at the bottom of the mouth. We were instructed to sit with a mirror in front of us, trying to get our tongue in the right place.

I decided to take extra classes in phonetics and pronunciation. The teacher who offered them was the "movie star" woman who taught us the first class. In those morning classes, when she was entering, we would say to each other, "Come on guys, straighten up. Here comes the movie star." After all, she spoke only Spanish so we could talk freely in English. I took the classes in the afternoon from her for three months. At the end of the last class she asked me in perfect English, "And how is your wife today?" I gaped. All the things we had said ran through my mind, and I apologized. She said, "Oh no, don't apologize. You men were so sweet." Nearly all the teachers in the school were adept at English, but because of the rule to speak only Spanish, they didn't use their English.

The year in Costa Rica was great for learning about and adjusting to the Latin American culture. We missionaries were told, "You will never change the culture. Your job is to preach the gospel, teach the Bible, and watch God change people's lives."

Traveling on buses was part of our adjustment to the culture. There were two kinds of buses. The cheaper ones were always crowded, and riders faced the danger of having their pockets picked or purses snatched. In the higher priced buses, everyone paid for a seat. No standing passengers were allowed. The custom was to pay the fare for friends, especially women, when they got on the bus. Both types of buses left at regular intervals, so it was easy to get to and from language school or downtown. I always took a taxi to and from the market to carry my baskets full of groceries and supplies, since baskets were not allowed on the bus. Taxis were an economical way of traveling, a lot cheaper than buying and maintaining a private car.

Ruth's late uncle, Gladstone Franklin (nicknamed Bub), established a Baptist church in the section of San José called Barrio Lujuan, that we attended. I preached my first message there in Spanish six months after entering language school.

We often visited Aunt Claudia. Her house was small but comfortable, built of wood with clapboard siding. The only furniture in her front room was several rocking chairs set in a circle. This Latin American custom meant that everyone faced everyone else in fairly close proximity. Aunt Claudia also introduced us to Latin food, including plantains (cooking bananas), rice, beans, yucca (manioc or cassava root), and the fruit of the country such as mangoes, papaya, and others. This was a big help in our adjustment to the foods of the Amazon River in Peru. Claudia was a cheerful, kind woman who diligently served the Lord in her church.

Costa Rica is a beautiful country. We often took bus trips on Saturdays to visit volcanoes and parks. We were able to approach the Irazu Volcano at close range. It had a big crater with an "eye" in the center from which steam always rose. We walked into the crater close to the eye and looked down 900 feet (274 meters) into boiling, roiling water at the bottom. That was where the steam came from. We also visited the more active Poaz Volcano. Its big crater was filled with sulfur fumes, so we didn't go down into it. On these trips we saw Costa Rica's lush farmland. With a range of weather from the tropics to the cool mountains, farmers are able to produce a wide variety of food.

Ruth was pregnant when we arrived in Costa Rica, but was able to attend most of the language classes. The Latin American Mission ran La Clinica Biblica, a hospital in San José, where Dr. Cameron from Winnipeg, Manitoba, practiced. However, Ruth needed regular injections of vitamin K to build up her blood. A medical missionary taught me how to give the injections, and had me practice on an orange. It was difficult for me to give Ruth her first shot. Just the thought of pushing the needle into her made me ill. But there was no other alternative, so I did it. Since then, I have given hundreds of shots, including ones to Ruth and our children.

When I took Ruth to the hospital on May 11, 1958, for the birth of the baby, the doctor told me I didn't need to stay, so I headed home to care for our boys. After giving them lunch and getting them settled for their afternoon nap, I left them with the housekeeper, Amelia, and headed back to the hospital. When I walked in, I asked Ruth how things were going. She smiled and told me Kathryn Ruth had been born. She was a tiny girl, just five pounds, 10 ounces (2.3 kilos). The doctor said everything went fine and she was a healthy baby. So now we had a Costa Rican member of our family. In later years, her brothers used to call her their Costa Rican volcano because she reacted so strongly to their teasing.

About six weeks after Kathy was born, we were eating supper when I heard a strange noise from the bedroom where Kathy had been sleeping. I rushed in to see what was going on. Kathy was lying on her back, bent over to one side. I picked her up and found her stiff and inflexible. She was curved around my hand in a "C" shape with her head bent to the side and her legs bent underneath in the same direction. I could move her back and forth and she wouldn't relax at all, yet her muscles weren't hard. I phoned the pediatrician who had checked her just a couple of weeks earlier. After hearing Kathy's symptoms, he came out to our house. He checked her over thoroughly, lifting her up, putting her down, feeling her muscles and doing everything he could think of. He said he had never seen anything like this. The doctor searched in his medical books to see if he could find a clue as to what was the matter. He found nothing. The doctor was well trained in his specialty, but he advised us to have Kathy examined in a children's hospital when we returned to Canada.

Kathy came out of that "spell" after about an hour. It appeared she was fine and completely over whatever strange medical condition she had. However, 28 days later, Kathy had another "spell" lasting about the same length of time. A month later, she had another one. This time, Ruth was standing in the kitchen doorway holding Kathy while talking with Amelia, who was standing about eight feet (2.4 meters) away with a frying pan in her hand. Kathy suddenly vomited right across the room into the frying pan. She then came out of the spell. This happened every month during our time in Costa Rica, with each spell lasting a little longer.

CHAPTER FOUR

Interlude in North America

When Ruth and I finished language classes the middle of December, we prepared to return to Canada. We needed to get Kathy checked and also raise more financial support. Aunt Claudia traveled with us to visit family in Canada. We flew into Miami and had a four-hour wait for our flight north.

In those days, each airline had its own waiting room and terminal for passengers. The exit to the planes was a large, high door that slid up so the waiting room was open to where the planes were loading and taking off. We were sitting near some suitcase storage lockers waiting for our next flight. Our two boys were running around playing and Kathy was in her mother's arms when suddenly we noticed Tom was missing. We were concerned because he could have gone out to any of those planes. We began looking for him, as did the air terminal personnel. They radioed out to planes that had taken off asking if there was a little boy on board who wasn't supposed to be. All the answers came back the same, "Negative."

About 15 minutes passed with no sign of Tommy. We didn't know what to do. I went back to where we had been sitting. I thought maybe he was hiding. I hollered his name as loud as I could. One of the doors of a suitcase locker on the second level opened and he said, "Here I is, Daddy." He was playing in there the whole time.

I went to Philadelphia to report to the ABWE office on our year in language school while Ruth, with Aunt Claudia and the three children, flew to Toronto. At the Toronto airport, Tommy disappeared again. A search had gotten under way when a pilot came in, holding Tommy by the hand. Our son had gone back out for another look at the plane. We learned on this trip to watch our children closely as we traveled.

Kathy had another spell on February 26 while the doctor was examining her. We took her to a pediatrician in Brantford who advised admitting her to the Sick Children's Hospital in Toronto. On March 19, we took her there, returning after three days to pick her up and get the test results. The doctor in charge of her case told us cheerfully what the problem was. He said, "She is full of Mexican jumping beans." During her three-day stay, Kathy had wrecked a crib, and broken a bottle and a few other things. Then the doctor grew serious. After a series of tests, the medical staff still did not know what the problem was. The conclusion was that Kathy's condition was genetic. The doctor did not know whether it would clear up or not. There was nothing he could do to help her.

Then the question arose: Should we go to Peru, considering Kathy's medical condition? ABWE's president, Harold T. Commons, consulted with Dr. Lincoln Nelson, ABWE missionary doctor in the Philippines. Link's opinion was that if nothing could be done for Kathy in North America, we might as well go to Peru. She probably would be no worse off there than in Canada. So we made plans for our trip to Peru. Kathy's "spell" on February 26 was her last. Perhaps Satan had sought to use our concern for little Kathy's health to divert us from going to Peru.

We still needed $50.00 a month support and $2,000 for our Outfit and Passage account. This is the account from which travel and set-up expenses are paid. We prayed and informed our churches of our need. After we brought Kathy home from the hospital, I received a telephone call from mission headquarters.

Harold Commons and Bob Burns were on the line. They told me Ken and Harriet Beard, from Mayville, Michigan, had promised $50.00 per month support. They also told us that almost all the needed funds had been donated for our Outfit and Passage account. We were cleared to go to the Peru as soon as the remaining $80.00 came in.

Ruth and I weren't able to meet our new supporters in Michigan before we left for Peru, but they supported us faithfully throughout our missionary career. We met them on our first furlough and were grateful to God for this fine couple.

The last Sunday in March we were invited to the morning service at Keelesdale Baptist Church, in Toronto, where our friend Don Gorrie pastored. Just before the morning service, we had prayer in the pastor's study and then turned to go out to the platform. Pastor Gorrie said, "Wait a minute! I have something for you." He reached into his pocket, pulled out an envelope, and handed it to me, saying, "There is $80 in this envelope." He named the woman who gave it. She was over 80 years old and suffered from arthritis. Yet she had taken a night job, cleaning offices, so she could earn money to help send us to Peru. God supplied the final $80 we needed. How humbling to have our needs supplied through God's faithful servants, sacrificially and, in this case, painfully given.

CHAPTER FIVE

On to Peru

On April 8, 1957, we said farewell to family members in Brantford, as Ruth's father drove us to the train station in Hamilton, 30 miles (48 km) away. Several people were there to see us off. It is the only time I ever saw Ruth's father cry, as he said goodbye to us and to his grandchildren. Tom, the first grandchild, was always special to his grandfather.

We set out by train for the ABWE office in Philadelphia. Our first stop was Buffalo, New York, where we changed trains. I had $400 in traveler's checks in my pocket. We already had our tickets, so this money was to pay for expenses along the way to Peru. In the Buffalo train station, I tried to change one of the traveler's checks. They wouldn't cash it in the station, so we got on the train with about $10 in Ruth's purse. We traveled through New York State to Johnson City, New York, and stayed overnight with our supporters, Dr. Bill and Maureen Foster.

The next day we headed on to Philadelphia. We traveled quite a distance, then had to change to another railroad line. We took a taxi to a station on the other side of the city. I asked the driver if he would accept a traveler's check. He refused. We scraped together all the cash we had, even digging into the corners of Ruth's purse. We were able to find enough for the fare, most of it in coins. The cab driver was not happy when I dumped them into his hand.

The commuter train to Philadelphia did not have many empty seats, so I had to sit with Tom and David a few seats ahead of Ruth, who held baby Kathy. The supper hour came and the boys were hungry. I said, "Let's all head to the dining car to get something to eat." I put my hand into my pocket for the traveler's checks, but they weren't there! I looked in all my pockets and in every corner of our bags. They were gone. I felt foolish and a bit desperate. What do you do in a train filled with people you don't know and with two hungry boys who don't understand there is no money? We hadn't brought snack food because we figured we could buy food on the trains.

I silently cried out to God, "Lord, we won't get to Philadelphia until 9:00 tonight. Guide me as to what I should do." Then the idea came that when the boys asked for food, I would take them to the water fountain and give them each a glass of water. Every five to ten minutes when the boys asked for food, I took them back for a glass of water. Intermingled with this were visits to the bathroom. On one of those potty trips, the train stopped at a station. When I got back to our seats an older woman was seated by the window. I sat down with Tom and David on my knees. They began playing with their toys. Out of the corner of my eye, I could see the woman looking at my sons. I thought, *They are cute little boys, that's why she is looking at them.* Suddenly she said, "You're a missionary, aren't you?" I looked at her in amazement. She laughed and said, "Oh, you can pick them out a mile away." She had been a missionary in Chile for 27 years.

We chatted for about 20 minutes, then the train slowed down. She said, "Oh, here is my station." During our conversation I did not mention our need of money for food, and the boys didn't ask for anything to eat. When she got up to leave, she shook my hand, leaving $10 in it before hurrying out. I didn't get her name, nor do I remember the names of the stations where she got on or off. Some day, I look forward to seeing her in heaven and thanking her for her gift, as I thanked God for her boarding that train. She left enough money to buy the boys something to eat *and* take a taxi to the mission house from the train station in Philadelphia.

The first thing on the agenda was to report the loss of our traveler's checks. We went to the main American Express office. Within 20 minutes I had the replacement checks, and can emphatically repeat the old advertisement: "Don't leave home without them."

While we were in Philadelphia, the mission office received word from the shipping company that the mattresses we ordered did not arrive in time to be loaded with our shipment to Iquitos. The only mattresses available on the Amazon in Peru were ticking stuffed with straw. We very much wanted those foam rubber mattresses. Missionary treasurer Don Drake suggested we put the mattresses into large duffel bags and take them with us as excess baggage. He pointed out it would be cheaper than sending them in a special boat shipment.

I phoned the shipping company in New York to tell them I would arrive the next day to pick up the mattresses. The man I talked to told me the warehouse would be closed, as the next day was a holiday. He suggested leaving the mattresses at a wine store just around the corner. The manager of the store agreed to receive the mattresses, as long as I picked them up by 9:00 a.m., store opening time.

I borrowed a car and headed early to New York City. There was little traffic, so it was easy to get to the wine store before 9:00. On arriving, I found several men sitting or standing nearby waiting for the doors to open. When the manager opened up, I saw the mattresses in wooden frame crates. I knew I couldn't carry them in the car that way. The store manager handed me a rusty hammer with the claws broken off. I went to work, hammering apart those crates. As fast as I put the boards on the sidewalk, men carried them away. The manager said, "They'll sell them for wine money." Eventually, I had the one double mattress and four singles rolled up and crammed into the car. On the way back to Philadelphia, I bought six large duffel bags and stuffed the mattresses into them. The airlines accepted them as baggage and, as they were light, we weren't charged much overweight. On arriving in Peru, the customs men, seeing my wife and small children, decided we were going camping and needed those mattresses. They cleared them right through without any import duty. So Don Drake was right; it was cheaper to take the mattresses with us.

At four in the morning on April 14, 1957, we boarded the flight from Miami, Florida, to Lima, Peru's capital, on the line that charged the least. What we didn't know, on making the reservations and paying for the tickets, was this line used two-engine DC3's, common in South America. Our plane landed in Honduras, Nicaragua, Panama, and Ecuador, before reaching Lima. At each stop we had to deplane and wait, so the trip took all day. David had a stuffed monkey with a long tail. He sucked on that tail instead of on his thumb. By the time we had arrived in Guayaquil, Ecuador, the tail was quite short. In the hurry out to the plane, the monkey was left on a chair in the waiting room. David learned fast to do without it.

And what happened to the traveler's checks? When we arrived in Iquitos, on the recommendation of veteran missionaries, we opened an account in a local bank. About six months after we arrived, I received a letter from American Express asking for the name and address of my bank. I sent this information, wondering why American Express wanted it.

Two months later, a messenger from the bank ran to our house, all out of breath, saying, "You are needed at the bank, right away!" The bank office workers sat at their desks in a large area behind the counter. The manager sat in the middle so he could keep an eye on everyone. I told the man at the counter who I was. He looked at me strangely, then went over to another man and whispered something to him. They both looked at me as they approached their manager. They leaned down, said a few words to him, and pointed to me. By this time, all the workers in the bank were looking at me. I had the strangest feeling I had committed some criminal act. The manager solemnly walked toward me with papers in his hand. He laid them on the counter and asked me if that was my signature. I looked at the papers. There were my lost traveler's checks! Someone had cashed them at different businesses in Buffalo, using an entirely different signature from mine. Perhaps my pocket was picked at the train station in Buffalo. I was summonsed to the bank to certify whether the signature on them was mine or not. This I did at a notary public, and that was the last I heard of the stolen checks.

CHAPTER SIX

New in Peru

We stayed in Lima for a month to complete the paperwork for our entry into the Amazon region. We lived in one room in a boarding house and ate in the dining hall, but the boarding house owner had little patience with children. There was no place for them to play, so we often had to go to parks or other places to get them out from under our feet. When I was away one day, David stuck his head between the bars in the window and couldn't get it out. Then Kathy put her head through the bars of her crib. About that time, the owner of the boarding house suggested the Greenslades find another place to live.

We moved 25 miles out of the city to a vacation center called Huampani, built for Lima's middle-class working people. There was plenty of room for the children to play, and the food was good. With good bus service into Lima, we had no problem getting in and out of the downtown area. We celebrated Kathy's first birthday at Huampani.

With all our documents in hand, we flew to Iquitos, Peru, over the Andes Mountains. Since it was a clear day, we flew through one of the main mountain passes, with impressive peaks rising on each side. When clouds cover the peaks, pilots have to fly over the mountains rather than between them. At such times, oxygen is supplied through tubes we placed in our mouths.

Looking down on the jungle canopy reminded us of a patch of broccoli. The winding rivers were the color of coffee with cream. Then came our first fleeting look at Iquitos as the plane flew over. Our first impression was of numerous rusty-tin and thatched-roofed houses. As we deplaned, the hot, humid, musty air hit us like a sledgehammer. ABWE missionaries in Iquitos met us at the airport. Bill Large, a fellow student at London Bible Institute, helped us gather our baggage and get into a pick-up truck. He drove us to the house he had rented for us, a two-story building surrounded by high walls with a big enough yard for the children to play in. Instead of glass in the windows, there were shutters that opened up to give the house an airy feeling.

At our request, Bill had furniture built for us. It was all in the house awaiting our arrival. The furniture was made either of tropical cedar or mahogany, built in local style and finished in a deep red color. We had to have six inches cut off the dining room table legs so it would be the height we were used to.

Since we carried our mattresses with us, we were able to sleep in our house from the first night. Missionaries loaned us linens and other items we needed. We weren't able to prepare our own meals since our stove and other equipment was still in customs, so we ate in various missionary homes.

Our house was located right across the street from the central market. We didn't have far to go to buy our food, but there were distinct disadvantages. The market opened at 4:00 a.m. as vendors arrived to set up their stands for the day. Radios were turned on full blast. Ruth and I slept in an upstairs bedroom, which meant the noise blared in on us early in the morning. The main station they listened to was Trans World Radio from the Caribbean, which had a clear signal in those early hours. At least we had good gospel programs to listen to when we were awakened so early.

The city of Iquitos is the furthest inland ocean port in the world. Freighters from the Atlantic arrive without the need of canals or locks. Iquitos is the main trading center for the whole jungle area of Peru. The only way in and out is by air or by boat;

no roads connect it with the outside world. Immigrants from Spain, Portugal, other European countries, and China generally owned the city's commercial businesses.

Iquitos had only six blocks of paved streets at that time. The main section of the city had a sewage system, but open ditches ran down the middle of the side streets. A good water system supplied the central part of the city, but we didn't drink tap water without boiling it first—the water was not always treated sufficiently to get rid of all the intestinal parasites and other things found in river water.

The buildings were of southern European style. The park in the center of the city boasts an all-metal building designed by the builder of the Eiffel Tower in Paris. The building was built for the world's fair held in Paris in 1900. After the fair, a businessman had it taken down and shipped to Iquitos, where he rebuilt it to house the main grocery store of the city.

This store did not offer fresh fruits and vegetables, but we could buy canned cheese and butter shipped in from Australia and New Zealand. Powdered milk came from Denmark in 58-pound cans. Flour came mostly from Canada. It arrived on the store shelves three to four months after being milled in Saskatchewan. When we bought it, weevils were already forming. We sifted them out through a fine brass strainer. Rolled oats came in sealed cans shipped by the Quaker Oats Company. That was the only cereal we had for breakfast during all the years we lived in the jungle.

The city's one ice cream parlor, the Favorita (the Favorite) offered delicious homemade ice cream in the flavors of jungle fruit. One month after our arrival in Iquitos, the South America Shipping Company opened a store that sold frozen foods and ice cream bars from the United States and England.

Three fresh food markets stocked local and imported foods. Beef and pork were readily available. Butchers simply cut whatever chunk of meat we wanted off the carcass. Potatoes, carrots, cabbage, and celery were flown in from the coast. These items were expensive but gave us variety in our diet. We mostly ate local food: rice, beans, plantains, yucca, and a variety of fish. Ruth and I had to develop a taste for most of the tropical fruit. Our children, on the other hand, liked the fruit right away. When we returned to Canada, they didn't like apples, strawberries, raspberries, and other fruits of our home country.

Our first Sunday in Iquitos, we needed to decide which church we would attend. The closest church, a block and a half away, was Peruvian Union, a member of the Association of Baptist Churches of the Jungle. Fellow missionaries warned against going there because the church had a strict rule about the length of a woman's hair. The church also opposed women having perms and curling their hair. Ruth's shoulder-length hair was wavy from a permanent. But this was the closest church to us, so we decided to try it.

Church members welcomed us joyfully, and the pastor and his wife hurried to receive us. They asked Ruth right away if she could play the organ. She answered she could, and they asked her to be their organist. We asked about her hair. They replied, "There is no problem with your hair." What the church people opposed was short hair frizzed up like sheep's wool. Ruth played the organ, and we had an active ministry in that church over the next few months.

In the South American countries where ABWE serves, each field council is responsible to handle its own business and methods of incorporating new missionary personnel. The Upper Amazon Field Council, of which Ruth and I were now members, decided new missionaries needed a full orientation program during their first months in Peru. The idea was for new missionaries to travel to different churches and ministries, getting to know the big picture before settling down in a particular spot.

At that time, the Association of Baptist Churches of the Jungle had three churches in Iquitos, three on the rivers, as well as numerous preaching points. Ruth and I were assigned to visit all of these. This meant traveling either in small speedboats or in the new mission launch called ABEM (the initials of ABWE in Peru) down the Amazon River 300 miles (485 km). Then another trip 250 miles (402 km) up into the Marañón River, followed by the final trip of over 430 miles (692 km) up the Ucayali River.

The Marañón and Ucayali join 125 miles (210 km) upriver from Iquitos to form the Amazon River. At the point where the rivers meet, the Amazon River is one and a half miles (2.5 km) wide. The Amazon often divides into smaller channels formed by islands which the fast currents create when the river rises and falls. We had to know which channel to take in order to avoid traveling farther than necessary.

When we first started traveling on the Amazon, experienced people who knew the river and the channels went with us. Later, ABWE missionary Don Bond gave me a unique river map he had drawn on rolls of bandages torn from old bed sheets donated by a Women's Missionary Society. The map marked the course of the Amazon and Ucayali upriver from Iquitos, with its channels and villages along the way. We slowly unrolled the bandages until we arrived at our destination. The map charted 430 miles (692 km) of river and kept us from getting lost.

Roads in the Amazon basin are difficult to build and maintain because the river basin has no rocks or gravel. During the heavy tropical rains, dirt roads wash out easily. So the rivers serve as the "roads." People travel by launches large and small, by dugout canoes, or by fast motorboats.

The current on the Amazon River is fast on the outside of the curve and slower on the inside. When traveling upriver, it is best to keep to the inside of the curves to take advantage of the slower current. Traveling downriver, it is best to keep to the outside, where the current is faster. This way you can arrive at your destination sooner, but there are dangers to beware of. On the outside of the curves, frequent large whirlpools can overturn even a large boat. The inside of the curves hide mud and sand-bars. The best course is to stay far enough from them that the boat does not run aground. When the river is rising or falling, there is always the danger of debris in the water damaging a boat's propeller. Large trees, branches, and even water lilies and weeds have tangled up or broken many propellers.

The Amazon water constantly carves out the riverbanks on the outside of the curves and builds up islands or sandbars on the inside. When the banks erode, large trees fall into the water. It is necessary to keep far enough away from these banks so falling trees do not hit the boat. As the river falls because of the lack of rain, many of these trees get embedded in the mud and sandbars. When the river rises during the rainy season, water covers these trees. This creates an unseen danger. Hitting a tree can puncture a hole in the bottom of the boat and sink it to the bottom of the river.

Swimming in many places on the Amazon is dangerous. Large catfish grow up to 8 feet (2.8 meters) long. If a boat sinks and the occupants try to swim to shore, these catfish can grab the unsuspecting swimmer for a special meal. In shallow water next to the sandbars, flesh-eating fish such as the *carnero* and *piranha* make their home. The latter will attack only when they scent blood, so we swam with them often. The former, however, attack at any time. People who live along the Amazon know where it is safe to swim. We followed the local people's lead and swam only where they did.

I made my first orientation trip with ABWE missionary Jerry Russell, traveling downriver to the mission station at Transvaal, established by Bill and Elva Scherer in 1932. They located in this spot to evangelize the area Indian tribes. The Scherers' house had been built on a high bluff on the banks of the Amazon River, and was visible for miles out on the river. It was a little over one mile (1.5 km) from the town of Pevas, located at the mouth of the Ampiyacu River.

Jerry and I headed up that river to visit two churches established many years before by the Scherers and pastor Joaquin Silva from Iquitos. The first church we went to, in the village of Pucaraquillo, was made up of Indians from two tribes, the Borras and the Huitotos (pronounced wee-toe-toes). Before they heard the gospel and turned to Christ, those two warring tribes were fierce enemies.

The Borras were known as ceremonial cannibals. When they captured a man from another tribe, they kept him in their village, waiting to hold a big reunion called a fiesta. The captured man did not try to escape. He believed life wasn't worth living if his own tribe wasn't strong enough to rescue him. When the fiesta day arrived, the villagers killed their prisoner and roasted his flesh. The leaders of the tribe would eat some of the roasted flesh, then go behind a bush and put a stick down their throats to vomit. This demonstrated to the other tribe that their people were no better than monkeys, as the captors ate their prisoner the way they would eat a monkey.

Those days of cannibalism were long gone by the time Jerry and I visited Pucaraquillo and joined the prayer meeting in progress. The next day we traveled on up into the Yaguas Yacu River to visit the Borra Indian believers in the village of Ancon. Those church members met in a building used for communal meetings, which was large enough to seat at least 300 people. The room was built of poles cut from the jungle and covered with a palm-leaf roof. High hardwood posts supported the structure. The building had been enlarged by a lean-to on each side. The chief, his two wives, and children lived at the far end of the building opposite its main entrance.

Upon arrival, Jerry and I headed up the bank to the communal building, where the chief greeted us warmly. Then he went to the side of the building where two logs were inclined at an angle. These were the *manguare* (man-guah-ray) drums used to call people. Each log was about seven feet long, and three and a half feet thick (2 meters by 1 meter), hollowed out almost completely with the topside open. The chief stood between the logs and hammered on them with homemade rubber ball hammers. The drums sounded musical, exactly one octave apart. About an hour after the chief beat on the drums, people began arriving. Canoe after canoe kept coming for three or four hours. The first canoe-load of people climbed up the bank, greeted me with hugs, then asked, "Where is Jerry?" This scene was repeated when each canoe arrived.

Jerry and I asked the chief, "How do people know who would be there when they arrive?" He answered, "I told them on the *manguare*." We had a hard time believing he could beat out our individual names on the drums. We asked for a demonstration with Jerry's name first, then mine. Amazingly, each sounded different. The chief claimed those drums could be heard for a three-hour canoe ride's distance.

The day after the services, as I talked with the chief, I noticed a young woman standing next to me. She stood about waist high on me, and was measuring her feet next to mine. Of course, hers were less than half the length of mine. All the women giggled at the sight. Then they took a string and measured my waist, which wrapped around three of them, and laughed some more. They called me "Goliath."

My pants had an elastic band at the back and a cloth belt on the front. The Indian women had never seen pants like that. They decided they wanted to find out how they were made. I felt a tug on my pants and reached around to grab them. The women were talking excitedly. I pulled up one side. They pulled down the other. I thought they were going to take my pants right off, and struggled to keep them up. Once the women figured out how the pants were made, they left me in peace—pants and all.

The Borras cultivate poisonous yucca from which they make a type of bread called *casabe* (caw-saw-bay). They harvest the yucca, peeling off its hard skin, then wash it and place it in leaf-lined pits. They cover the peeled yucca with leaves and dirt, leaving it there for three days to ferment until the root is soft and mushy. Then they place it in a woven grass press that resembles a large snake. They pack that so full it bulges, then hang it up with a weight on one end. This squeezes out the poisonous juice. What is left is an edible pasty mass. The last step is scooping the mass into low, flat pans about three feet across and placing the pans over hot coals to bake. The result is a large cake about an inch thick. It is quite tasty when it is fresh. Our family ate a lot of *casabe,* but after only one day, it gets hard and tastes stale.

Back in Iquitos, Bill Large, director of the Iquitos Baptist Bible Institute asked me to teach a course on church discipline. This was the start of many years spent teaching and training national leaders. Since Bill wanted me to get to know the students, he invited me to attend their annual picnic held on Padre Isla (Father Island). This island was located offshore from Iquitos where the Amazon River divided into two channels. Students organized a soccer game on yet a smaller island beside Padre Isla. I wanted to see the canoes and boats tied up along the bank, so I didn't join in the game right away.

In looking over the boats, I noticed the bottom of one of the largest ones was a rounded dugout canoe enlarged by overlapping planks. I dove under the boat to see if it was the same shape on both sides. As I came up on the other side of the boat, I felt hair brush against my arm. I pulled up the hair and was shocked to find an eight-year-old girl at the end of the hair. I assumed she was dead, but grabbed her around the waist and squeezed hard. Water shot out in a torrent from her mouth. Apparently she wanted to join the students on the small island, but was soon out of her depth in the channel. I carried her to the bank, squeezing more water out of her lungs. Finally she began to cry. Her mother ran down the bank shouting, "Pasiona, why did you disobey me?" She picked up a three-foot-long, one-inch-thick fibrous shell from a jungle fruit and began whipping the girl. I felt sorry for Pasiona, but the beating helped her get rid of more water. She survived and later attended the Bible institute, married one of the graduates, and is a pastor's wife today.

Two days after the picnic, Bill Large and I traveled up into the Marañón River to visit the town of Nauta. This was my first trip in this speedboat, which I later bought, a 14-foot runabout with a 30 hp Johnson outboard motor—"our car" for river travel. On June 26, 1957, I set foot in the town to which God had called my wife and me. Bill and I headed farther up into the river, then returned to Iquitos to a special celebration for Ruth's and my fifth wedding anniversary.

The following month Ruth accompanied me to Transvaal, 150 miles (241 km) downriver from Iquitos. In a letter to her parents, Ruth wrote:

> Kathy stayed with Richard and Ruth Gray, ABWE missionaries in Iquitos, while we were on our ten-day trip. We left Iquitos for Transvaal at 5:00 a.m. in the mission launch ABEM that was loaded with seven-and-a half tons of cement, lumber, and a big old refrigerator, among other things. We carried this for David and Maver Heibert, the ABWE family stationed in Transvaal. We arrived just at dark, around 6:00 p.m. Tom and David loved the trip. They have been playing "boat" ever since. The launch is easy to steer. We took turns doing this. There are a lot of whirlpools, making the back end of the launch feel like it was riding on slippery ice.
>
> On Sunday we attended the morning service in the village of Pevas. A 19-year-old man accepted the Lord as Savior. Every service we go to, no matter where, you have to hop in a boat and travel by river. There are no roads whatsoever. All the houses are built on stilts, many of them with no walls, only a thatched roof. People sleep under mosquito nets.
>
> In the afternoon we went by speedboat to Pucaraquillo, about an hour's ride. After the service, Ivor and David Heibert got out their medical kits and did lots of doctoring. The women, including a 12-year-old-girl, sit in the service nursing

their babies. We returned to Transvaal in the dark. It isn't enjoyable traveling with just a flashlight in the dark in a speedboat because of the floating logs and the debris in the water.

The next morning we went with the Heibert family to visit the Borra Indian believers at Ancon on the Yaguas Yacu River, about a seven-hour trip by launch from Transvaal. We stopped on our way at a little place where two missionaries from Wycliffe Bible Translators work, to deliver their gasoline and kerosene. We arrived at Ancon at suppertime and began getting our meal ready. The bank was soon full of curious Borra Indians, old and young, with their little kerosene lamps, peering in through the windows of the launch.

When we arrived, the chief banged on his drums, calling folk from along the river.

About 50 people, including children, gathered. These Indians, up in the jungle far from missionaries and organized churches, are happy when someone comes for a service. Ivor played a tune on a saw. He didn't have a violin bow, so he banged out the notes with a little stick from a toy xylophone set. They thought that was something out of this world (and it was!). Maver Heibert sang with him so it would at least sound like a tune. Then I played two or three accordion solos. Afterwards, the women would look at me, giggle, and make their hands go in and out as if they were playing. Maver and I went down to the boat and put the children to bed. We slept in a row in the launch, all 11 of us, nine on the floor and two in hammocks.

In Ancon, as each family arrived, they claimed a spot inside the big building. Women hung up hammocks for their babies in the lean-to section. Each family built a small fire on which to cook. In preparation for the service, men placed sawed-off logs in a circle for everyone to sit on. The women with babies sat in hammocks all around the lean-to. Pedro, the spiritual leader of these Borra Christians, turned to David Heibert and said in broken Spanish, "You, and you, will preach." He turned to me say-

ing, "And you, you will lead the singing." Most of the singing was
in the Borra language, but they requested we teach them songs
and choruses in Spanish. The Indians wanted to learn all the
Spanish they could so they could interact with the Spanish-
speaking traders.

The service started at 6:30 in the evening. We sang for 40
minutes and David preached for 45 minutes. After the service,
Pedro told us some babies needed medical treatment. David
brought out his medical kit and we gave some injections and
treated others. This went on for about half an hour. Then Pedro
turned to me and said, "And you, you are going to preach." He
turned to David and said, "And you, you are going to lead the
singing." This was the second service, which lasted a little longer
than the first one. After the service we chatted, visited, and gave
more injections. Then they started their prayer meeting. Everyone prayed at the same time for about 15 minutes. Afterward,
there was more visiting followed by another service. After midnight, we excused ourselves and went down to the launch to
sleep. We didn't know at that time these services had replaced
their former dance fiestas, so they expected them to last all night.

At first we traveled without motor controls at the front of
the boat. Somebody would duck back to regulate the speed and
shift the motor. On our return trip down the narrow Yaguas Yacu
River, we were moving along quickly with all of us standing near
the helm. We swung around a sharp curve. Right in front of us,
the full width of the river, was a bunch of large dead trees floating in the water. There was no way to avoid hitting them. I
charged back to the motor to switch it into neutral and then
reverse to stop the boat. I slipped, slamming my foot against the
motor mount, breaking my little toe. I accomplished the shift so
we didn't hit the trees, but my toe throbbed badly.

The only medicine David Heibert had for pain was a capsule
used in hospitals to calm patients before taking them into the
operating room. I took one and got sleepy. You are supposed to

take these pain pills about every six hours. After four hours, my
toe started hurting again, so David gave me another capsule.
Although I was in charge of the boat, I don't remember docking
in port at Transvaal nor heading to my room. I went to sleep at
4:00 p.m., and slept right through until 8:00 am. That night, a
boat arrived loaded with bricks and cement. They couldn't get
me awake to help unload.

On the following day, David Heibert, Antonio Castillo (a
national pastor from Pucaraquillo), and I left Transvaal to go
downriver to the leprosarium at San Pablo. We decided to try a
shortcut, a narrow channel on the inside of an island. That was a
mistake. The channel was too shallow for us to continue on and
too narrow to turn the launch around. We tried backing out. In
doing this, the end of the rudder arm snapped. With the steering
mechanism broken, we could no longer steer the launch. The end
of the rudder arm needed to be welded in order to hook it back
onto the shaft. The closest place to do this was at the leprosarium, a full day's travel downriver. Dave Heibert said, "We'll have
to wait for another boat to come along to tow us." In that section of the river, other boats might not appear for several days.
We asked God to send a boat soon.

I put my farming background to good use. On the farm we
learned, out of necessity, to fix things with pieces of wire, wood,
and nails. I applied this experience and replaced the metal steering arm with a four-foot wooden two by four, nailing a large
crescent wrench on it. I fitted the adjustable jaws of the wrench
to the square top of the upright shaft, wiring it firmly in place.
Then I took the steering cables off the metal arm and nailed
them to the other end of the wooden arm. This replacement
took us downriver to the leprosarium, where the metal arm was
repaired.

About 90 believers attended the church at the San Pablo leprosarium. For fear of infection, we were not allowed to shake
hands with the believers or make contact with the things they

used. Special chairs were taken down from the rafters for visitors. The leprosy patients did not use these chairs. The pulpit was extra wide, with one side for those with leprosy, the other for visitors. After the service, the pastor showed us around the leprosarium, taking us to the various wings of the hospital. In one we saw people with advanced leprosy. A blind woman, who was also completely deaf, sat on the floor rocking back and forth, singing, "Jesus Loves Me, This I Know." The pastor told us she had been a believer for many years and was thankful to God for His love and salvation. She could respond only to touch, which we weren't allowed to do.

This leprosarium is now used only for people who become disfigured, which is rare these days because of the medicine available to treat leprosy. With the use of medication, most patients at the leprosarium were declared symptom free. They moved across the river, formed their own village, and established a church. They still serve the Lord faithfully in that section of the Amazon River. The pastor, who lost all his fingers because of the effects of leprosy, regularly paddled his canoe to other villages to preach the gospel, resulting in converts whom he gathered in groups to worship and fellowship together. They continue serving the Lord, and ABWE missionaries and pastors in the region regularly visit them.

CHAPTER SEVEN

The First Trip to Nauta

The children rapidly adapted to the Peruvian culture. Tom saw women carrying pots on their heads, so his main ambition became to do the same. He would put banana leaves in a pot and try to carry it on his head. Then he tried putting water in the pot. He usually spilled it and ended up playing in the mud. Of course, David always tried to do the same.

When we arrived in Iquitos, we were given a small dog called Happy. It had curly hair and was white with brown and black spots. When Ruth played her accordion, the boys and Kathy would march around singing. Happy would put her head back and howl. The parrot would chatter and the monkey, which almost sounded like a bird, accompanied the group. One day Happy was barking furiously. Ruth went to see what the excitement was about. She saw a four-foot poisonous snake in the walkway by the house. I killed it with a broomstick. Happy earned her keep that day.

Our next orientation trip was to Nauta, starting on August 14, 1957. We were excited about arriving as a family in the town where we would live. We traveled on the ABEM with two Christian men from Nauta at the helm. They knew the river between Iquitos and Nauta well. Ruth wrote to her parents:

> We went down to the port of Iquitos in the evening to sleep on the launch. The ports are usually at the bottom of a high bank, with either no steps or steps cut out of the dirt, which most of the time are muddy. I made it almost to the

boat when my foot slipped into the slimy mud up to my ankle. It was after 11:00 p.m. when we finally got to sleep. We started out at 5:00 a.m. and stopped at a small village called San Fernando at 5:30 p.m. and slept in the boat. Ivor visited around a bit.

We left again at 5:00 a.m. and arrived in Nauta at 9:00 a.m. The river was low so we had to dock the launch far away from the regular port. We walked a mile through mud and sticks on a path by the river and through trees before we reached the mission house. Believers from Nauta carried all of our things to the house.

The children had a great time running through the large empty mission house and walled-in backyard, where there are several fruit trees and sugar cane. In Nauta there are no roads, only paths in the streets. Most of the houses are very simple. Some are just poles with a roof and no walls. The church is built national style, with wooden walls, a tin roof, and a dirt floor.

We stayed in Nauta for two weeks and took part in a meeting every night but one. The first Sunday I got up enough nerve to take my accordion to the evening service. I played with one hand, as I am still learning to play it. They have no musical instruments, so it didn't matter to them if I played that way. A lot of people came to listen, and we had a large audience around the windows. After the service, we all went to a sick man's house to sing. They asked me to play some more. Most of the people who had been at the service followed us to the house and came in to sing and hear me play. My arms were tired after this, as the accordion weighs about 30 pounds. One night I took it to a service in one of the believer's homes. There were about 50 people standing outside listening. Another night we had a business meeting at our house till 12:30 a.m. They disciplined three members and talked quite a bit about schooling for their children.

There were two deacons at the church, one of whom was named Luis. His father was on his deathbed. We went over every evening after the service to sing and pray with him. He said it made him feel closer to God. He was 70 years old and had been saved just the year before. He asked Ivor if he would marry him to the woman he had lived with for many years. They had four grown children. He knew he was going to die soon and wanted to be right with the Lord. This was Ivor's first wedding in Spanish. The woman stood by the bed with the man propped up on pillows. He was groaning and moaning in pain the whole time. He told us that up until a year ago, he had literally served the devil. We came to love him in the Lord. All the time we were there, his son, Luis, was building a casket for his father. His father died shortly after we arrived back in Iquitos.

During November 1957, I joined Dave Heibert, Jerry Russell, and Jorge Inuma on the launch for a trip up the Ucayali River. Our first stop was a four-day convention of Baptist churches at Bagazán. Delegates gathered to discuss matters of mutual concern and encourage one another in the faith.

After the convention, we left on a pitch-black night to continue our trip. This was my first river experience traveling on a dark night with no stars or moon showing. I found that on such a night a soft light always glows on the water. Once your eyes become adjusted to it, you can see debris on the water. When you get to know the river well, you can swing around a curve into pitch blackness with confidence there is nothing there you can hit.

The launch had a 35 hp diesel inboard motor, but was made so an outboard motor could also be fastened on the back in case the inboard broke down. Behind this was the toilet, sticking out over the water. On this dark night, Jerry Russell was sitting on the spot. David, Jorge, and I were at the front of the boat, with Jorge steering. I looked out and faintly saw what looked like two large logs with a channel of water between them, which Jorge was heading for. I thought, *He's a river man; he knows what he's doing.* It looked as though we could slide between them.

We soon found out it wasn't two logs but one big log with the middle part under the surface of the water. At night, that middle part didn't show. The base of the launch's hull was a dugout canoe with a rounded bottom. It had an unusually deep keel which sloped down 18 inches (46 cms) below the bottom of the boat. The hull curved up front and back. The metal keel at the back was quite long, forming part of the propeller and rudder brackets.

We hit that log doing about 12 miles (19 km) an hour. The front end of the launch went up so far that I thought it was going to stand on end. With the momentum and the roundness of the hull, the launch slid right over the log. Down went the front end, up went the back, then after the keel passed the log, the launch plunged into the water which shot up through and over the toilet. Jerry got soaked. After the launch settled down to normal, Jerry said, "I thought I was on a rocket going into orbit, then in a submarine about to submerge." We kept on going. After all, we had passed the log.

We stayed that night to present the gospel in Requena, the largest town on the lower Ucayali River. We asked the town authorities for permission to hold a service in a small park where a large cross was located. After supper, we went up to the park and Jerry began playing his accordion. Soon a large crowd gathered. They enjoyed the music and our singing. We took turns preaching. Then I offered tracts to everyone. People rushed toward me from every side. Jerry grabbed his accordion and hurried to the outer edge of the park. When people pushed in against me, crying for tracts, I held them high over my head and began dropping them into the crowd. When the tracts were gone, we gave some New Testaments and talked with a few individuals. We learned later that the religious authorities in the town demanded the people turn in whatever literature they had received. They obeyed out of fear, and all of it was burned in the park. This was my first exposure to religious efforts to prevent the spread of the gospel. The town was known among the religious authorities as "the Athens of Peru." They boasted that no evangelical would ever establish a church there. Today, there are two Baptist churches in that town.

Our last stop was in Tierra Blanca, where ABWE missionary Edna Hull lived with a national Christian worker. We wanted to make living a bit more comfortable for the women. We installed a chemical toilet and dug a drainage ditch so water wouldn't stand in her yard. Again, my farm experience in Alberta stood me in good stead. I had helped my father lay out ditches for irrigation and I knew how much a ditch should drop.

Edna wanted to prepare a meal of pork and beans for us, but she didn't have any of the latter. Painstakingly, she got out a game played with beanbags and removed the beans. She cooked up her special dish and served it to us. We enjoyed it and expressed our appreciation. The next day when we set out on a trip upriver, Edna went along. Mealtime came, so she checked through our food supplies. She found a good quantity of cans of pork and beans. We lived on these the entire trip to Tierra Blanca. Her reaction was, "You guys! You let me do all that work taking the beans out of the bags and didn't say a thing." Truthfully, her dish was better than what we ate from the cans.

With the trip to Tierra Blanca, the Greenslades' orientation was finished. It had been a year of introduction, learning, travel, newcomers' sicknesses, adjustments, and blessings. We traveled over 5,000 river miles (8,000 km), visited all the established churches and groups in formation, and surveyed many towns and villages where there was no gospel witness. The established churches—some strong, others weak—encouraged and challenged us. The need for evangelism and strengthening the believers was overwhelming and sometimes depressing. Ruth and I needed prayer for continued strength and wisdom.

CHAPTER EIGHT

Ruth's Reflections on Nauta

After four years of dreaming, our family arrived in Nauta in February 1958. We were not tourists looking forward to returning to familiar things in our own country. We were there to stay, entering into the adventure of living and adapting to our new surroundings. This was our new home. We would work with believers in the Nauta Baptist Church and learn how to be missionaries.

Nauta is located six and one-fifth miles (10 km) from the mouth of the Marañón River, which joins the Ucayali River to form the Amazon. The town was founded by the Cocama (Co-caw-ma) tribe, led by the famous chief Manuel Pacaya, and was officially recognized in 1830. In 1842, it was declared capital of the district, and in 1943 became the capital of Loreto, the largest province in area in Peru. In Spanish, the term *nauta* means "someone who navigates." However, the name may have come from a large earthen vessel called *mauta* in the Cocama language.

Ivor and I were the only English speakers, forcing us to use our recently learned Spanish. I was afraid to speak Spanish because I knew I was making mistakes, but the people were patient, helping us many times. There were no paved roads or vehicles, not even bicycles. The little park in the center of town had a sidewalk, but much of the time it was covered with un-shelled rice drying in the sun. Most of the houses were built of material gathered from the jungle. There were shutters on the windows, but no glass or screening. Roofs were made of either tin or woven leaves.

The local people owned very little furniture. Often their beds were a wooden platform. The whole family slept in a row, each under his or her mosquito net. Many houses had dirt floors, others cement. Sometimes when we went to visit, a cackling hen would run out of the bedroom after laying an egg under the bed. Some houses were built on stilts, because at certain times of the year the river rose and flooded the area. During the hottest part of the day, animals gathered under the houses to stay cool. If a cow decided to scratch its back on one of the stilts, the whole house swayed.

A river launch hauled our belongings from Iquitos to the port. Men carried our goods to our house by strapping them on their backs. One of our trunks was filled with books and weighed 410 pounds (186 kg). Four men helped load it on a man's back. He slowly carried this heavy load up a steep bank and then three blocks to our house.

Peruvian men are short in stature but have muscular legs and strong backs. I enjoyed being taller than most of the women. At school I was always the shortest in my class.

We lived in a large adobe house built 100 years earlier. It had a tin roof, cement and wooden floors, and screened windows, which meant we didn't have to sleep under mosquito nets. A high brick wall surrounded the large backyard. The workshop, shower room, and small schoolroom stood along a side wall. Our stove, refrigerator, and iron all used kerosene (drawn from a barrel by sucking hard on a hose). When the kerosene reached our mouths, we quickly put the end of the hose into the tank. Sometimes we were a little slow—and got a mouth full of kerosene!

Fruit trees such as banana, lemon, papaya, and apple-pear grew in our yard. The apple-pear tree has broad leaves, grows tall and is shaped like a Christmas tree. Ivor warned our boys never to climb it. One day, as he entered the yard from a side door, he saw the branches moving at the top of the tree. Suddenly four-year-old David came rolling down from branch to branch as he tumbled through. He grabbed the bottom branch, swung down, dropped to the ground and walked away as if nothing happened. We were relieved he landed safely, but after his punishment he never did that again.

Some people wonder about the wisdom of parents taking their children to a tropical country. When they think of the jungle, they imagine snakes, spiders, bugs, savage Indians, and other dangers. Some of these dangers exist, but God is our great protector. The safest place in this world is in the center of God's will and in the place He wants us to be. We found this to be true for our children and ourselves.

Dr. Arieta delivered Elizabeth Ann (Betty) in the Iquitos government hospital at 2:00 a.m., December 31, 1958. The doctor let me leave the hospital in the afternoon if I promised not to sweep any floors or do any heavy housekeeping. We stayed in one of the student dorm rooms at the Bible institute, which was on summer vacation. We found a baby's crib for Betty, who was not yet one day old.

Bill and Ruth Large lived on the upper floor of the institute. We slipped upstairs for five minutes to greet them and then headed back down to our room. As we entered, we saw what looked like a piece of red hose near one of the walls. Ivor asked, "Where did that hose come from?" Then the hose began to move. It was a brilliant red snake about three and a half feet long, which had entered the room through an inch-high space under the door. It moved toward Betty's crib. Ivor ducked out of the room and found a short stick. Then he hurried back and killed the snake, which was already climbing the leg of the crib. People of the jungle say snakes are attracted by the smell of milk and will stick their heads into a baby's mouth. As Ivor hit the snake with the stick, it jumped off the crib leg and landed at his feet. We did not know at the time that this snake was not poisonous, but I was glad Ivor successfully killed it.

Betty was a light blonde. When she was a few months old, she lost most of her hair. The Peruvian women worried she would never have hair again. Their babies are born with lots of long black hair and never lose it.

Tom and David, like typical boys, liked to tease their sisters. A favorite trick was to catch big, soft frogs and throw them at the girls. We had to teach them not to do this, as Peruvians have a superstition that if a girl touches a frog she will never have a baby. One night when Ivor was away, I tucked the children in bed and blew out the lamps. When I checked on them later, I saw a fat frog jumping around in their room. David had put it in a tin can under his bed. I never knew what I would find in his pockets when I washed his clothes: dirt, bugs, or worms.

Ivor traveled often on the river. He and men from the church would go to villages to hold services. I stayed in Nauta with the children, sometimes for several days or weeks. Ivor would say he would be home on such and such a day, but many times he didn't arrive until later because the motor broke down, or it was too stormy to travel on the river in the speedboat. Each time his father was gone, Tom had nightmares, and it was hard to get him to sleep again. Ivor's being gone so much was hard for me, too, at first, but the Lord helped me overcome my fears. When Ivor was away, the believers took good care of our children and me.

I home-schooled Tom in a small room behind the house while the other children played in the yard. One day, one-year-old Betty was playing in front of the door of this little school-room where I could keep an eye on her. I could hear Betty chatting away to herself. Noticing a change in the tone of her voice, I quickly glanced out to see what was happening. Betty was reaching for a large tarantula spider moving towards her. I was able to snatch her from the danger and later killed the spider.

We caught rainwater off the roof and stored it in tanks on

the side of the building. The water was always colder than the air; it made for a refreshing shower in that hot climate. After showering one day, I saw a movement out of the corner of my eye as I reached for the towel—a big black tarantula. I praised the Lord for protecting me from it.

Peruvian women were interested to see how we foreigners lived. Our bedroom window looked out on the street. Only the bottom half of the window was curtained so air could circulate through the top half. Sometimes a woman climbed up on the wide outside sill to peer over the top of the curtain. One time we heard a blowing noise. We looked and saw one corner of the curtain was swinging out. A woman was blowing the curtain in and quickly peeking. We would go to the door and invite the woman in to have a better look. Often women came to visit for hours, just watching what I did. They were fascinated by how I opened a can, peeled the vegetables, diapered the baby. This was new to them, as their babies were sufficiently dressed with just a little shirt. Their reasoning was "Why put diapers on when they'll just get them wet?"

We had several pets. A beautiful turquoise macaw, wild ducks that walked in step like soldiers, two or three dogs, some chickens, always a small monkey, and a talking parrot. We sometimes named our parrots Aurora, as it is easy for them to say. Poor Aurora! We finally had to give her away because she insisted on chasing Kathy and Betty and biting their feet. They would scream and the parrot would stand there and laugh and laugh, then turn around and say, in Spanish, "Goodbye for now."

The Baptist church was located across the park and up the street. The benches had no backs, so it was dangerous to fall asleep during a service. Sometimes this happened, however, and the sleeper would fall onto the floor. I always tried to get to church early so I could sit next to the wall and have something to lean on. The men and boys sat on one side, the women and girls on the other. Mothers laid their babies on the floor in front of them and flapped a towel up and down over them to ward off the mosquitoes. For this same reason, people rubbed their feet against each other, as some didn't wear shoes. At first it was hard for Ivor to concentrate while preaching; it seemed everything was moving. But he soon got used to the motion. The building had no electricity, so we placed small, open-flame kerosene lamps on shelves around the room and on each side of the pulpit for the evening service. The church also owned a kerosene pressure lamp, and, when it worked, we used it. We strung wires across the building and hung curtains to separate the Sunday school classes. This kept the children from watching the other classes but did nothing for the noise.

We bought our food at the town market. Once in a while, they had a side of beef hanging up. We bought a few kilos and cut it up in usable pieces. It was always tough, so I tenderized it by squeezing papaya juice on it. Ivor had to go to market at 4:00 a.m. in order to get the meat he wanted. Our main diet was fish, rice, and beans. When we got tired of that we ate rice, beans, and fish. We learned to eat plantain, manioc, turtle stew, alligator tails, monkey meat, and many other things.

My ministry was with the children and women, several of whom couldn't read. I wanted to train some of them to teach Sunday school. Felicia was willing to learn. She could read but never stopped for any commas, question marks, or periods. She just kept reading until she ran out of breath. I taught her the rules of punctuation. She soon could read well, but she had never learned to write. She solved this by having her 12-year-old son write down what she was to say. Then she could read and teach the lesson. She became a very good teacher. I later taught her and other women how to write. Some of them had never held a pencil in their hands before. I taught them this skill. At first they were so nervous that their hands shook.

Most of the women sewed their own clothes, as there were no clothing stores. They enjoyed learning new techniques. I told them to save all the little pieces of leftover material and taught them how to make a tied quilt. I also taught them to knit babies' booties, bonnets, and sweaters.

Norma, a teenage girl, helped me take care of the children and worked in the kitchen. One day I smelled a terrible odor from the kitchen. I checked the stove, and found a pan full of flying ants roasting in the oven. She said they tasted good, and her people considered them a delicacy. We didn't try them, fearing the taste was as bad as the smell. I told her not to put them in the oven again. The next time flying ants landed in the yard, she caught them, pulled off their wings, and ate them raw. We took Norma with us on one of our trips into Iquitos. She had never seen a car, truck, bicycle, or taxi, and became confused, as she didn't know which was which. She was interested to learn that the moon in Canada is the same as the one in South America.

A young man named Jorge Inuma helped Ivor with the boat. One day Jorge was carrying the outboard motor on his shoulder down the bank to the boat. He slipped and went right into the river, completely submerged. Soon he appeared, climbing up out of the water with the motor still on his shoulder. Ivor asked him, "Why didn't you let go of the motor and swim out?" Jorge replied, "I don't know how to swim." The weight of the motor made it possible for him to walk up the bank; Otherwise, he would have drowned.

A young couple in the church fell in love and planned on marrying, but the girl's father strongly objected because of the groom's racial background. Her father threatened to disown her if she insisted on the wedding. Late one night, Ivor and I heard a knock on our door. It was the young girl, holding a suitcase. Her father had kicked her out of the house and told her if she married the young man, she was never to come back. The couple decided to go through with the marriage.

This was the first wedding ever held in the church. The people of Nauta had never seen a Baptist wedding before. I played

"The Wedding March" on a portable pump organ, so-called because I pumped the foot pedals to send air through the reeds. The church was filled to capacity, with many other people standing outside, hanging in the windows, and perched up in trees. Even the local priests showed up to see what was going on. The wedding was a wonderful testimony to the whole town. The groom worked at the bank; he later became manager of the bank and the pastor of the church.

After the wedding, when the new bride met her father in the street, he ignored her. Ivor said, "Wait until your first child is born. He will want to see his grandchild and will begin talking to you." That is exactly what happened.

One day I was ironing clothes in the kitchen during a heavy rain. I didn't think I needed to stop my work because the iron was heated with kerosene. Suddenly, a loud crash of thunder was followed by a burst of lightning which came in through the window and struck the cement floor beside me, burning a little hole. I wasn't harmed at all, and again marveled at God's protection.

CHAPTER NINE

Spiritism and Spiritual Growth

Early one morning, two men from the Nauta Baptist Church and I set out at 4:00 a.m. to visit a church in the village of San Fernando. We floated downriver in a canoe. I sat in the middle of the canoe; deacon Luis Freitas sat behind me, and church member Emilio Rengifo sat at the front. They were doing the paddling. There was no moon, but the stars shone brightly. The river was calm, although eddies swirled as the Marañón River flowed down to join the waters of the Ucayali. We heard jungle sounds from the nearby bank.

Luis asked me if I believed in the *tunchi* (toon-chee). To the folk on the Amazon, this is the evil spirit with a unique whistle who travels around at night to see whom it can frighten. I answered, "I hear the *tunchi* whistles at night." Emilio said, "Yes, it does; and not only that, you can call it." I had never heard the call and was skeptical. So I said, "Call up one." He answered, "All right, but we have to sit here quietly. After a bit we will hear one whistle, probably on the other side of the river. I will mimic it and then it will come toward us, whistling every few seconds until it is right over us. If it sees it cannot scare us, after about a minute, it will whistle about 200 yards on the other side of the boat."

We sat quietly. By starlight, I could see bats flying overhead looking for insects. I could also hear the sound of their wings. After a few minutes, a whistle sounded about a mile away on the other side of the river. Emilio mimicked it exactly. The whistle began coming toward us, repeating itself every few seconds. Closer and closer it came, until it whistled right above us. I sat there staring as hard as I could, trying to see what bird was making that whistle. After about a minute, it whistled 200 yards off to the side. On thinking about this experience later, I realized there was something different about the sound. The strength of the whistle on the other side of the river was exactly the same as the strength of the whistle right above us. There was no change in the volume. I have often heard this whistle since then, outside a church or while walking down a pathway. To the local people, this is the evil spirit which they fear.

Most people on the Amazon are animists. They believe souls can exist outside the body in dreams and visions, can be transferred from one body to another, and persist after the death of the body. They believe every inanimate object (such as a tree or a chair) has a spirit which can be offended.

When Jorge Inuma, one of the faithful church members died, his all-night wake was held in the church building. The custom was to hold two preaching services, the first at 9:00 p.m. and the second at 1:00 a.m. As I prepared for the services, five-year-old Tom told me his friend had seen Jorge flying by above the church. I realized this came from the belief that the soul of the dead stayed around town for 24 hours, and only departed when the body was buried. That night I preached on 2 Corinthians 5:6–9: *"Absent from the body, present with the Lord."* I assured the congregation that Jorge was not in Nauta.

Peruvians fear the witch doctor and hexes that might be put on them. They often get sick from this fear. They believe four different types of birds are the emissaries of witchcraft. If one of these birds flies through their house, it means the witch doctor has put a hex on those in the house, and someone will get sick. In such cases, the residents pay an herbalist shaman to counteract the hex or sickness. The belief is that a good herbalist can outdo any witch doctor, and it is true that some sicknesses are cured with herbs. The herbalist will call for two large pipes of tobacco to "smoke" the patient. He fills the room with a cloud of tobacco smoke as he touches the affected part of the body, all the while mumbling incantations. He may prescribe an herbal remedy, but the medicine is mixed with spiritualist practices.

People firmly believe in all this. It is often stated that these practices are found only among primitive people. This is not so, as it is common among some educated and professional people, even in North America. Wise is the missionary and pastor who respects people's beliefs and uses the Bible to illustrate God's power over all evil spirits.

We preached the gospel. As a result, Peruvians trusted in the Lord Jesus for salvation, and came to the confidence of eternal life. Their lives, families, and villages were changed for the better. We often received invitations from the authorities of towns and villages to send missionaries to them. The invitations usually read, "You make our towns a better place in which to live." Our problem was we did not have enough missionaries to go to all those places. This is still the problem. A great need exists for workers to be sent into the harvest.

We also trained church leaders. We taught them how to lead services, teach the Bible, and administer the church. The two deacons in the Nauta church preached and taught, and both Ruth and I also taught. But the Sunday school was growing so fast we needed more teachers. Also, we knew that when we moved after a few years, the church needed people to carry on the work. We held special classes to train the Nauta church members how to teach. Naturally, I used the teacher training courses I learned in Bible college. After six weeks, I realized the believers in Peru did not understand.

Then I had an experience that showed me how to train leaders. We needed a playpen for baby Betty to keep her from crawling around on the floor, where she could pick up intestinal parasites' eggs. We wanted a folding playpen that we could take with

us on river trips and into Iquitos. Deacon Luis Freitas was a furniture maker. Showing him the picture of a playpen, cut out of a
catalog, I asked him, "Can you make this?" After studying the picture, Luis asked, "Can you show me a model of what you want?"

I found a small box and cut the bottom flaps so they would
meet in the middle and fold up. I creased the sides so the box
would fold flat. Luis handled the box for a while, folding it in and
out. Then he said. "I can make that." Using this model, he made
a playpen out of mahogany that lasted us for years and is still
being used by a family in Iquitos.

With this, a light came on in my mind. Ruth and I were getting nowhere trying to teach Peruvians how to teach a Sunday
school class. We needed to show them a model. I asked Emilio if
he would teach a class of 12-year-old boys. He swallowed once,
twice, and then a third time, showing his nervousness. Then he
said, "I will do it; show me how." He was asking for a model.

I took Emilio into the class with me, telling him to watch
what I did. The next Sunday, I instructed him to write down
what the lesson was about so he could do a five-minute review
the following Sunday. He had seen how I did this, so he copied
the same format. After three Sundays, I invited him to our house
and taught him the lesson as I would in class. Then I told him he
would teach on Sunday. He prepared well, but while he was
teaching he paced nervously in front of the class. The boys moved
their heads, following his movements. After class, I complimented
Emilio on how well he had taught, then suggested that next time
he might try standing still while teaching. He thought for
a minute, then said, "I didn't realize I was doing that." Emilio
became a good teacher.

Over the years, Ruth and I taught many Peruvians by showing them how, then having them practice. Other missionaries and
pastors did the same. As a result, there are effective leaders and
teachers in Peru and Argentina.

Ruth developed music leaders. She taught them how to beat

out the time of the song, often taking the arm of the leader and swinging it the way it should be done. Whenever she told me someone in the church had a good voice, my response was, "Get him going." She would ask him to lead the Sunday school in one chorus he knew well. Then the next Sunday, she would have him lead two choruses. The following Sunday, she would add a hymn, until this man was leading the entire service. Then I would appoint him as leader of the Sunday school. The new leader nearly fainted until I pointed out that he was already doing it.

We watched in awe as the gospel brought changes into the lives of people such as Cesar, an eight-year-old boy. Members in the church visited his parents and invited them to church. They brought their children, but Cesar had a learning disability and didn't fully understand. He was afraid because the local priest told people that Ruth and I were devils. Cesar sat in Ruth's class and cried the whole time. This went on for five weeks. On the sixth Sunday, Ruth told me Cesar didn't cry and actually listened to the lesson. Later that year, we held an evangelistic campaign with Ricardo Panduro, a pastor from Iquitos. At the end of one of the services, Ricardo invited all those who wanted to receive Christ to go forward. Cesar was the first off his bench. He prayed to receive Christ as Savior. I asked him who now lived in his heart. He answered, "The Holy Spirit." He had understood the message that, on receiving Christ, we become temples of the Holy Spirit. One month later, Cesar's schoolteacher asked, "What have you done to Cesar?" I replied, "What do you mean?" He answered, "He learns now. It is easy to teach him." What an adventure to see such a dramatic change in a little boy's life.

We saw how salvation brings about social uplift. When people receive Christ as Savior, their lives change. The men become faithful to their wives and children. They no longer steal. They stop drinking and are able to work full days, earning more money. That means they are able to buy shoes and clothes for the family and a sewing machine for their wives. They fix up their houses. The change was often so notable that those who were not evangelicals accused the missionaries of giving the converts a salary. "How else could they get all those things?" The gospel leads people into becoming good, faithful citizens who provide for their families.

One day in the Iquitos Post Office, I met a Peace Corps worker who was a university student from the United States. I asked her, "What have you come to do in Peru?" She said, "My project is to go into the river villages to help the people form cooperatives so they can get better prices for their products." She was enthusiastic about her work. I wished her well, commenting, "They need all the help they can get." One year later, I met her again, but she looked downhearted and discouraged. She told me that at first her work went well, with three cooperatives established in three villages. All was going as planned, with the people getting better prices for their products. Then disaster struck. In the first cooperative, the president stole all the money. In the second, the secretary took off with the funds. In the third, the treasurer made away with all the assets. The three cooperatives folded. She said, "To help these people, you would have to change their hearts." I told her that was what my wife and I had come to do. I also said, "If there had been evangelicals in those key positions, the cooperatives would still be operating."

We also observed the Nauta church members practice biblical discipline a number of times. The church was careful to follow Scripture when believers strayed from biblical teaching. Generally, those who were admonished privately by the deacons responded positively, confessed their sins to the Lord, asked forgiveness of the congregation, and mended their ways.

One woman didn't. She was worried that her two teenaged daughters would not find husbands, since there were no bachelors in the church. She encouraged her daughters to attend dances in the town. The girls were inexperienced and open to being seduced into a sinful lifestyle. The deacons counseled this woman and her daughters, but they paid no heed. The woman publicly denounced the deacons in the street. Even unsaved people tried to get her and her daughters to change their ways, all to no avail. There was no change in their lives or repentance for the scandal they caused. So the members of the church obeyed the instructions of the apostle Paul in 1 Corinthians 5:4, 5: to *"deliver such a one to Satan for the destruction of the flesh, that his spirit may be saved in the day of the Lord."*

The girls' mother ignored this action by the church. Fourteen months later, she became ill. The doctor in Nauta sent her to a large hospital in Iquitos for an operation. I was in port the day she and her husband were about to leave by launch for Iquitos. I said to her, *"Hasta luego* (until a little while)," a common way for friends to say goodbye to those they expect to see again soon. The woman answered, *"Adios* (goodbye), pastor," a permanent farewell from someone you do not expect to see again. My answer was, "Please, it's just *hasta luego.*" She answered, "No, pastor, it is *adios.*"

The doctor in Iquitos told me the operation was successful but they couldn't wake the woman from the anesthesia. She died three days later. Her husband told me that just before she went into the operating room, she requested he ask the believers to forgive her for the wrong she had done. Then she told him she would not see him again on this earth. The whole town of Nauta knew of the church's discipline. They knew the woman died because of her disobedience to Scripture. After that, whenever believers began to stray, we reminded them of what happened to this woman.

CHAPTER 10

Boas, the Bishop, and Boiling Water

Our house in Nauta had a large yard with some fruit trees and a small palm tree. The area was blanketed with heavy, coarse grass. One day, our three oldest children, all under five years of age, were in the yard playing around the small palm tree, having a great time running and falling down in the grass. I hired Emilio to cut the grass with his machete. He swung the three-foot-long blade of the machete in a circular motion. He was moving closer and closer to where the children were playing. I was afraid they would move too close to the machete and get cut. I asked them to move to a tree on the other side of the yard. They did this, and Emilio continued to work toward the palm tree.

When he got close to the tree, Emilio stopped short. I called out, "What's wrong?" He whispered, "Snake." Running over, I saw a boa constrictor about four and a half feet long and two inches in diameter. This snake apparently had been there all the time the children were playing around the tree, but it never touched them. My first thought was, *Thank you, Lord, for your protection.*

I said to Emilio, "Kill it." He answered, "No, we should catch it so we can sell it in Iquitos for good money." I asked, "How do you catch it?" "Easy," he replied. He tossed down his machete (which I thought a foolish action), and moved toward the snake, coiled in a figure eight with its head up, ready to strike. Emilio moved his hand toward the snake, which struck but missed as

Emilio jerked his hand back. He repeated this two more times. After the third time, the snake was too tired to lift its head. Emilio grabbed it behind the head. It coiled around his arm, squeezing and relaxing every minute or so.

I said, "Let me try." Emilio threw down the snake, and I copied his action. The snake struck and missed as I jerked my hand back. After the third time, it was tired out, so I grabbed it behind the head. Emilio was right; it *was* easy. We kept that snake in a barrel until we could ship it to Iquitos.

When we first arrived in Nauta, we noticed the streets were unkempt, with weeds and brush covering them. People tired of walking through this and decided to do something about it. I was invited to attend the planning meeting. I wanted the streets cleaned up, too, and attending the meeting would give me an opportunity to learn more about the people and the town. The group in attendance formed two committees to organize the cleanup: one for each section of the town. They appointed a president, vice-president, and secretary, then named me as treasurer because they knew I wouldn't misuse or steal the money. I was working with others for the betterment of the town and fulfilling my social responsibilities.

Because of this, the sub-prefect (the civil governor of Loreto Province) and the new mayor of the town decided, without asking me, to include my name in the list of council members for the town and province.

I became aware of this appointment when reading an article in the Iquitos newspaper. One of the priests in Nauta was also on the list. My immediate reaction was to refuse the appointment because I didn't want to be involved in politics. I learned this was an appointment, not an election, so politics didn't enter into it. I also felt it might not be good to sit on the same council with a priest who openly opposed evangelicals. I prayed and thought much about this. A few days after returning to Nauta, a runner appeared at the door with a citation to an unofficial meeting at the mayor's house to organize the new Town Council.

Walking up to the mayor's house, I noticed the sub-prefect and the mayor in heated discussion. Their faces were red, and I thought they were arguing. Smiles broke out on their faces when they saw me. The mayor asked, "Do you know what that priest Julio did?" I answered, "No." The mayor replied, "He refused to accept his appointment." The sub-prefect added, "Because we named you to the council." To refuse their appointment was an insult to the men who made up the list. I silently said, "Thank you, Lord, for guiding me. You protected me from insulting these men." The council named me inspector of public works, the best position for learning about the government and politics of Peru.

Once a year the bishop for the Department of Loreto visited Nauta. The Town Council always held a reception for him, as the bishop is an official of the government of Peru. The Roman Catholic Church is a protected religion under Peru's constitution. As a council member, I received a citation to attend the reception. I consulted with the two deacons of the Nauta church. They said, "Go. The bishop always speaks against evangelicals in those receptions. Go and see what he has to say with you there."

The reception was set for 10:00 a.m. The council meetings always started at least a half hour late, so I showed up at 10:30. When I arrived at the priest's house where the reception was held, I found everyone waiting for me. I realized that Peruvians were not running the affair; the Spanish bishop and priests were. Since they are European, they are more time oriented than the relationally oriented Peruvians, to whom time is not very important.

When I entered, one of the priests leaned toward the bishop and whispered something to him. I knew he was telling the bishop who I was. I found the last available seat and sat down. The reception started with the bishop speaking for a half hour on the greatness of the Roman Catholic Church and how powerful it was in bringing about miracles such as those that occurred in the famous church of Lourdes. He said nothing about evangelicals.

After his speech, the bishop asked the sub-prefect, "What can I do for you and the province?" The sub-prefect read a list of needs, all of which involved money. The bishop told one of the priests, "Write down the requests." Then he asked the mayor, "What does the town need? That list, too, was written down. From there, he turned to the inspector of education and asked him, "What can I do to help in your department?" After receiving the three lists, he told everyone they would get all they asked for, letting it be known that he packed a lot of influence with the government in Lima.

Then the bishop stood. Everyone else stood and formed a line. I got into the line also, and watched what the 20 or so people before me did. The bishop held out his closed right hand, which most people took, bending down to kiss the big ring on his hand before moving on. Some, however, just shook his hand. I studied the difference, and soon saw that those who didn't work for the government shook his hand. Those who did kissed his ring. *Aha*, I thought, *those who shake his hand are business people. The Bishop can't touch them. Those who work for the government could lose their jobs if they don't show the Bishop they are faithful to the church, so they kiss his ring.*

When my turn came around, the bishop held his closed hand out to me. He was a big man with a big fist. I took his fist, forced his fingers open, grasped his hand, shook it, and said, "Mr. Bishop, we need to chat. I invite you to my home for tea this afternoon." He breathed out through his open mouth, jerked his hand away from mine, and extended it—closed—to the next person. He didn't say a word to me, although he spoke to all the others.

A few days later, in the first session of the Town Council after the reception, different council members spoke at some length about how wonderful it was that the bishop was going to get the town all the things and money it needed. I listened for some time, then asked to speak. The mayor recognized me. I asked sev-

eral questions, "Do you see the high school on the other side
of the park? To whom does it belong?" The answer was, "The
bishop." "Is it finished?" I asked. They answered, "No, because the
bishop doesn't have enough money to finish it." Then I said, "If
the bishop can't get enough money from the government to finish his own high school, how do you think he is going to get
money for our town and province?"

The council members realized the bishop's promises were
empty. Then I said, "I'll tell you how to get money for the hospital, the market, the hotel, the municipal offices, for paving the
streets, for running water, and for a sewage system. Send tele-
grams every week to the representatives and senators in Lima,
asking them to get us the funds we need. I'll guarantee they will
compete with one another so they will have something to boast
about in the next elections." My prophecy turned out to be true.

Our ministry was not only to the town of Nauta and the
Baptist church. Many nearby villages and towns needed the
gospel and two small churches needed encouragement. I began
visiting them, traveling with one of the believers from Nauta in
a 14-foot open speedboat.

The village of San Fernando had a group of believers from
two families, 25 from each. I often visited that group on Sunday
mornings. There I learned an important lesson that helped me in
all the following years. After teaching for one hour, José said,
"That was good teaching. Now tell us how to do it." From this
remark, I realized I needed to make my teaching and preaching
practical. I needed to tell the believers how to put the Word of
God into practice.

Tom accompanied me to the village of Bagazán, which had
an organized Baptist church. Leaving Bagazán, we traveled an
additional 45 minutes to visit a believer who lived in a village on
a tributary of the Ucayali River. This village was made up of
small farms with about 100 yards (91 meters) between each
house. The couple I wanted to visit lived in the last house, about

a mile (1.5 km) from the main river. Tom and I stayed overnight with them. Early the next morning, two policemen came out of the forest and warned the village that a group of savage Indians had camped a half-hour's walk further into the jungle that same night. These Indians had the custom of finding isolated houses, raiding them, killing the men and older boys, and taking the women and girls captive.

The moon had shone brightly through the whole night, which is when those Indians liked to travel and raid houses. However, they did not come near our isolated house. We thanked God for His protection, hurriedly packed our things, and headed back into Bagazán. On hearing the Indians were close to their town, people immediately cleared the forest for 165 yards (150 meters) all around the town. This was so the Indians would not have any trees to hide behind if they wanted to raid the town. This was the closest I got to the Indians who had the custom of killing a man as soon as they saw him.

Another village I visited was San José. A graduate of the Bible institute in Iquitos, Alberto Sepulveda, with his wife and children, had moved to this village to start a church. I went there to hold a week-long evangelistic campaign. A schoolteacher in town had been educated in religious schools from first grade right through teacher's college. She opposed everyone from any other religion than hers. She prohibited school children from attending our services. Those who did were disciplined the next day. She would make them kneel outside in the mud for as long as two hours. She also had the boys bring water from the river and keep a pot of water boiling on her open fire in the kitchen, telling the children, "This water is to throw on the missionary if he comes near my house or school." Alberto told me she was capable of doing so, as she had thrown boiling water on pigs and dogs that wandered too close. I didn't want trouble, so did not venture near her house or school. I prayed to the Lord and waited to see what would happen.

The third day into the campaign, a boy came running up to the pastor's house. He gasped, "The teacher sent me to ask the missionary to come and treat her sick baby." I asked Alberto, "What should I do?" He thought her request was sincere. People on the rivers knew that missionaries did medical work. I picked up my medical case and headed over to the school to see the teacher and her 10-month-old baby. As I listened to his chest and back, I realized he had pneumonia. He already had the bluish shade babies along the Amazon turn when they suffer from this disease. I told the teacher, "It will be difficult to save your little boy because you waited too long." I said, "I need to boil a syringe and needle to give him an injection." She said, "Put it in the pot of boiling water there on the fire." I smiled to myself, thinking God must be laughing, too, because that was the water she had threatened to throw on me if I went near her school. I gave the baby a shot of antibiotics. I followed this up with injections every few hours. The little boy got better.

One morning three months later, Luis Freitas, the deacon, looked worried as he came to our house. After chatting a few minutes, I asked, "What can I do for you?" He said, "I just heard that the teacher in San José asked her witch doctor father-in-law to put a hex on you in order to kill you." I thought, *Such gratitude for saving the life of her baby!* I had heard of hexes being put on people, but until now, no one had tried it on me. After talking about the hex for a few minutes, I changed the subject. Luis got the strangest look on his face. I asked him, "Now what's the problem?" He answered, "The hex, the hex. Aren't you afraid of it?" Then I realized how seriously he was taking this. I showed him from Scripture that the devil and his cohorts could never touch me unless God gave permission. I read to him from Job, chapter one, where the devil couldn't touch Job without God's permission. I pointed out that if God wanted to take me in that way, it was all right with me because "absent from the body" is "present with the Lord." This was a great relief to Luis. Word soon spread to all of the believers that the witch doctor could not touch them without God's permission. This gave them great confidence and took away their fear of the spirits and demons.

San José was known in the police logs as one of the most evil villages of that entire area. A few people were saved and, later, because of strong persecution, the converts moved across the river to establish another village and Liberty Baptist Church. They built a church building that could be seen for miles away.

When Liberty Baptist Church hosted a convention for the five churches and small groups of believers in the area, I was the special speaker. Attendance for the evening service was too large for the church building, so benches were set up outside. The full moon shone brightly on that lovely tropical night. Tall posts, placed on each side of the congregation, held kerosene pressure lamps. In addition, small, open-flame kerosene lamps rested on each side of the pulpit. I was preaching on the freedom from fear and evil we have when we know Christ as Savior. Suddenly the people in the back row jumped up on their benches. Each row did this in order, from back to front. A ten-foot boa constrictor slid out from under the benches and fled into the bush. Because people equate snakes with the devil, I had a good illustration of God's protection. The devil flees from those who trust God.

CHAPTER 11

Church Planting in Iquitos

When it was time for furlough in 1961, we packed up everything, although we expected to return to Nauta. Ruth wasn't feeling well. We didn't know at the time that she was pregnant.

We arrived at the Toronto airport at 3:00 a.m., on May 26, 1961. The only baggage that arrived with us was a small cardboard barrel in which we packed our curios from Peru. We were the last ones in line to go through customs. The Royal Canadian Mounted Policeman on duty took quite a while to fill out papers on Betty, who was born in Peru. The customs men asked us to show them everything in that barrel. The last thing they looked at was our blowgun. One of the customs' officers handed it to the policeman and asked, "Should we allow them to bring this dangerous weapon into Canada?" The policeman asked, "What is it?" When I told him, he just tossed it back and said, "Get out of here." So we didn't lose our blowgun.

Finally, at 4:00 a.m., we greeted Ruth's family members who had waited to welcome us. We crawled into bed at 5:30 a.m. When I woke up, the sun was shining brightly. By the angle of the beams in the window I calculated it to be around 8:00 a.m., and wondered why I felt so rested. I thought, *I'll let the rest of the family sleep late.* Much to my surprise, when I looked at the clock, it was 12:30 p.m. I was used to the sun being directly overhead by 8:00 in the morning. It isn't that way in Canada.

On this furlough, we lived in Brantford with Ruth's parents.

We averaged 4,000 miles (6,437 km) a month, visiting our 39 supporting churches and others, as we needed additional support. Ruth's father bought a 1953 Buick with an eight-cylinder motor for $350. It served us well, but some church people thought it extravagant for a missionary to drive a Buick, even though it was eight years old.

To us, the "jungle" of traffic in North America was worse than the jungles of Peru. For four years we had never traveled faster than 25 miles (48 km) an hour, and that was on water. For our first six weeks in Canada, we experienced dizzy spells. Our doctor told us we suffered from what is called "bushed," the same thing that happens to people who move out of the bush within North America.

A highlight of our furlough came on January 26, 1962, when daughter number three was born. We named her Karen Irene, after my twin sister, Irene.

During our furlough, we reported what the Lord was doing in Peru. We enjoyed this and were able to meet many wonderful people. We knew they would pray for us when we went back to Peru.

In August 1962, we returned to Iquitos. Bill Large asked us to teach at the Iquitos Baptist Bible Institute. Since the training of local people was essential for the ministry on the Upper Amazon, we accepted that opportunity, rather than return to Nauta.

Ruth picks up the account:

> Our first challenge was to find a house to rent in Iquitos. Few were available, so while we hunted, we stayed in the ABWE guesthouse. We finally found a place one block from the central park, in a row of joined houses next to an elementary school. Our house was separated from the classrooms by a high wall. There was no backyard, and the front of the house was on the sidewalk. But it was comfortable and, eventually, we got used to the noise from our neighbors.

While living in the guesthouse, eight-month-old Karen became seriously ill with vomiting and dysentery. We took her to a doctor who prescribed shots of penicillin. This didn't help, and she started swelling besides. The doctor himself became ill, so we took Karen to a pediatrician. As soon as he saw her, the doctor blurted out, "She's been poisoned!" After hearing her history, he changed his diagnosis to penicillin reaction. One more shot could have killed her. The pediatrician said, "Never give her anything containing penicillin." He prescribed an antihistamine to counteract the reaction and a chocolate-based powder to cut the diarrhea. He told us to feed her a spoonful of intravenous fluid every five minutes all night long. ABWE missionary Vivian Bond helped us. By morning, the swelling had receded from Karen's arms and legs, but she was very thin and her eyes had rolled back until only the whites showed. This frightened me, but the pediatrician assured me she was fine. Karen soon regained her health.

The kitchen in our house was four steps higher than the room where the washing machine, tubs, and shower were located. The door separating these two rooms was made of slats and had to be hooked so it would not swing open. Karen loved to scoot back and forth in her walker. One day, someone left the door unhooked and she flew down the steps, landed right-side-up at the bottom, and suffered no injury. God protected our children from accidents and dangers so often!

During furlough, I learned of successful evangelistic campaigns held in the Philippines through which many churches were started. I saw the need of helping the established churches in Iquitos reach out to the unsaved in their neighborhoods and offered to hold evangelistic meetings for them. The idea was to have each one last for four to six weeks, with concentrated personal evangelism carried out by church members.

The first campaign was during December 1962 in Bethel Baptist Church, where Ricardo Talledo pastored. The meetings were well advertised in the section of the city where the church was located. The pastor and I met with church members for prayer a few days before the campaign. They were enthusiastic and invited friends and relatives. We held services with the children at 6:30 and with the adults at 8:00 every night of the week except Saturday. I preached every evening and taught at the Bible institute each morning. During that month of meetings, 115 people made professions of faith.

The next campaign lasted five weeks during April and May of 1963 at the Belén Templo (Bethlehem Temple) Church. Joaquin Silva pastored this church, the oldest in the Association of Baptist Churches of the Jungle. Among the members, 35 people consecrated their lives to the Lord, and 27 people made professions of faith. During the campaign, 18 more were baptized and joined the church. Many of these were young people who had grown up in the church. I preached every night but was not able to finish the final week. The last Wednesday I began to feel a pain in my back, although I didn't feel it while I was preaching. After the service, the pain increased so I drove to the clinic.

The doctor came in wearing a sports jacket. After examining me, he said, "You have a very common disease of the region. You have pneumonia because you don't wear an undershirt. It is good you came in tonight; otherwise they would have been making your coffin in the morning." X-rays showed streaked lungs. The medical staff gave me a large injection in each hip. The shots hurt worse than the pain in my back. The doctor prescribed daily injections of antibiotics, sent me home to bed, and told me to stay there for two weeks. The Iquitos climate is always hot, so I wore only a sports shirt. Most of the time it was soaked from perspiration. The doctor always wore a jacket in the evenings because of the dampness of the climate. *Live and learn,* I thought. After that, I always wore an undershirt and often a jacket.

With each series of meetings, we learned how to do things better. We started our first campaign at Bethel Baptist Church without proper preparation in prayer, training in personal evangelism, and follow-up. Six months later, only two converts out of 115 still attended church. This was a big disappointment. During the campaign at Belén Templo, there were fewer decisions but all continued attending the church. We later realized the difference was that all those who made decisions at the Templo had already been evangelized by church people. More time was spent in preparation through prayer and training the members.

One week after my prescribed two-week bed rest, we started a six-week campaign at the 28th of July Church. The church had this unusual name in commemoration of Peru's independence day, July 28. Preparation for this campaign included prayer meetings in homes and at the church. During the first week, we held classes on soul winning. Another week was spent studying the religious beliefs of the people of Peru, to help believers approach their relatives and friends with knowledge. Another week was dedicated to a missionary conference. The pastor, Ricardo Panduro, baptized eight people during the meetings. All of this resulted in a rapid growth for the church. When we started, the average attendance was 80. In three weeks this went up to 137. It continued to grow through a regular visitation program, reaching 160 in a few weeks.

Tom went with me to a campaign with Don and Vivian Bond in Tierra Blanca. Tom had fun swimming with Steve Bond. One day he fell out of a canoe with his clothes on. He could swim well enough to grab on to the canoe, but decided it wasn't easy to swim with shoes on.

We traveled back to Iquitos on a large river launch, the *Huallaga* (wah-yaw-gaw), named after a jungle river. There were 300 passengers on board. Tom and I slept in the passageway on the top deck beside the cabins and behind the wheelhouse. We lay on a blanket and covered up with a sheet. I put our suitcase in front of our heads as a windbreak. The chilly breeze generated by the boat's movement is very cool and damp on the rivers.

I gave the gospel to several people on the *Huallaga*. One high society woman from Iquitos was especially interested. I explained to her that Christ is our high priest and that salvation is not by works. Although she did not make a decision for Christ, she decided she would never use the rosary again nor pray to St. Veronica to help her.

I helped Belén Templo hold a one-week missionary conference, the first for this church. During the conference, the church was encouraged to reach out to other parts of Peru. The church set a goal of 1,000 *soles* a month (about $40 in U.S. currency) in missionary giving, a large sum for these people whose income was low. The faith promises doubled the goal. What excitement that brought to the church. Two widows who made a living washing clothes by hand, were overheard saying, "Remember, this faith promise is over and above our tithes." The church people kept up their faith promises each month and began supporting three of their own national missionaries.

There was a need to strengthen the Association of Baptist Churches of the Jungle with a good base of churches in Iquitos. In the early 1960s, there were three organized churches in the association, 21 unorganized groups, and several preaching points. Jerry Russell and I surveyed the entire city of Iquitos to see where new churches were needed. As there was no city map available, we purchased a blueprint from City Hall. We placed 12 red dots on this blueprint, by faith marking the spots where we thought a new church ought to be established. We began praying and planning how to achieve this. Ten years later there were 11 churches, all within one block of each spot we marked.

In answer to the challenge of establishing new churches, Ruth and I decided to reach a section of the city known as the *Arenal* (the sandy place), adjacent to the Iquitos Baptist Bible Institute. We estimated the population at 6,000 to 8,000. We organized Bible institute students into teams and held a Vacation Bible School, where several children were saved.

We began in April 1964. Our initial team consisted of Ruth

and me, our children, a Bible institute graduate (Vidal Villacorta), and the house-to-house visitation teams from the Bible institute. We sent the students out two-by-two each Friday and Sunday afternoon. The idea was to make friends first, then present the gospel.

On the first visitation day, I took Jorge with me since he was the most fearful student. We went from door to door, searching out people whose hearts God was touching. At the third house, a man invited us in and said, "Evangelicals? I have been waiting for you for 27 years." He told us that when he was 12 his parents took him to the town of Yurimaguas on the Huallaga River. One evening he heard a missionary preaching on a street corner. This North American missionary talked about heaven and how to go there. The next day the family returned home. The man continued, "Ever since, I have wondered about that message, wanting to go to heaven when I died. Tell me, how can I do this?" We carefully presented the way of salvation. He received Christ as his Savior and came to the assurance of eternal life. He still serves God in a church on the Tiger River in Peru.

We visited another house, where a woman named Zoila was sitting at her open window working on her sewing machine. We chatted with her and she accepted our offer to return the next Sunday for a Bible study. She was quite staunch in her own faith, yet had visited other religious groups searching for something to satisfy her longing for a closer relationship with God. We concentrated on presenting Christ as our great High Priest. This interested her because she went to confession at least twice a week. During our hour and a half Bible study, she went back again and again to emphasize she had her own priests. I emphasized that we can approach Christ to confess our sin at any time, any place, and that He never gets sick and never tells us to come back next week because He is too busy.

We returned the next Sunday to find a birthday party in full swing next door. Zoila's house was one of a row with only a thin partition separating each one. Most of the rooms are open at the top and have no ceilings. Zoila sat me in a chair next to the wall of the neighbors' dwelling. Just three feet on the other side, a bass drum thundered away. Zoila sat about six feet from me with the young student, off to my left. The noise of the drums and flutes was so loud we had to shout. Later, the student said he thought Zoila and I were fighting. Again she emphasized her priests and I made my emphasis on Christ as our great High Priest, ready to forgive all our sins and give us eternal life.

After about half an hour she shouted, "You say that Christ, the great High Priest, will forgive us of our sins and give us eternal life. How does He do that?" I shouted back, showing her from the New Testament how we have to believe Christ wants to forgive us of our sins, that He will forgive us of our sins, and that He is waiting for us, by faith, to ask Him to do it. When she heard this, she shouted, "I want to do it." So that day Zoila came to know Christ as her Savior.

Through the visitation program, a number of people like Zoila were saved and needed nurturing in biblical truth. We met a man who had been saved through the work of Harry Stahlman, one of the earliest ABWE missionaries in Iquitos. As a young man he made several preaching trips on the river with Harry, but had wandered away from the Lord. He repented, and later became a deacon in one of the Baptist churches in the city.

It was time to gather these people together so they would get to know each other, be strengthened, and be taught the Word of God. We arranged to start a Bible study in one of the believer's homes. The institute students invited the new converts and took them to that home. When Jorge and I went to get Zoila, she told me she didn't think she could go because the only dress she had was the purple one she wore in commemoration of Christ of the Sacred Heart. I told her that was no problem, and suggested she put it on and come with us. She wore the purple dress, belted with a white cord and a little Sacred Heart on the front. Under her arm she carried her Bible, hymnbook, and chorus book, which she had already purchased. We caused quite a stir as we moved through the streets. About 50 people were following us by the time we got to the home where the Bible study was to be held. They stood outside and listened. One man loudly objected, but was unable to come up with persuasive arguments against the Bible's teaching.

We continued the Bible classes, and in answer to prayer, there were professions of faith nearly every week. By July, we had two Sunday schools each Sunday morning, one at 9:00 a.m., the other at 10:30 a.m. Together they averaged 50 to 60 attendees each week. The house where we held Sunday school couldn't hold any more than this number, so we prayed for a place to meet where we could combine the two groups and begin weekly services.

One week Jorge and I visited Emma Tulumba. Emma readily accepted our visits and we began teaching her the way of salvation. After five visits, she came to know Christ as her Savior. She grew rapidly and soon faced the issue of her statues, which she regularly knelt before in prayer. It was a great day of victory when she got rid of them. This came about through hearing the clear teaching in Scripture of not bowing down to idols.

We continued to teach Emma every Sunday afternoon. She was married, but I never saw her husband those first weeks. He worked as a garbage collector, but was almost constantly drunk. One Sunday afternoon, I heard stirrings in the room on the other side of the partition near where we were sitting. Then Emma's husband, Jesús, came out and sat beside her. We learned he had been in the adjacent room every Sunday afternoon, sleeping off the effects of Saturday night. When he heard us talking, he would wake up and listen. So he had heard all the teaching Emma received. He came out because he was ready to receive Christ as Savior, which he did that afternoon. This brought a big change in his life. He stopped drinking and attended our services regularly.

Six months later, I asked Jesús if his old drinking cronies ever tried to get him to drink again. His answer was, "Pastor, they don't even know me." This startled me but, as I gazed at his face, I realized that over the intervening months his appearance had changed completely. He had gained weight and the signs of drunkenness disappeared. No wonder they didn't know him!

Our groups had been meeting in different homes for Bible studies, but none was large enough to hold a service for everyone to meet together. I mentioned this to Emma one day. She said, "Here is my front room. You can meet here." The room was about 13 by 25 feet (4 by 8 meters), so we met there for our first combined services. All who attended were new converts except for my family and Vidal Villacorta.

Most of the women and some of the men could not read or write. We knew they learned from memory, so we sang the same hymn five times instead of singing five different songs. By the time the service was finished, people went home singing the song.

By November 1964, attendance had grown to 120 in Sunday school, partly because a group of believers from a downtown church joined us. Jesús and Emma's living room was overcrowded. One Wednesday, when I went to their house to prepare for the service, I found Jesús taking out the partition between the front room and their bedroom. I asked him, "Why are you doing this?" He answered, "Oh, pastor, we need more room for the services. We will sleep in the kitchen and you can have our bedroom. This way, the work can continue to grow."

We organized the church in April 1965 with 25 baptized members and three deacons. The people chose the name Emanuel Baptist Church. Ricardo Panduro, an experienced and capable man, was named pastor. In May, when the church was one year old, we bought four lots across the road from Jesús and Emma's house.

By July 1965, the church had gathered enough money to buy material for a meeting place. We started building a portable tabernacle in the yard of our house. It took more than three months to dry the wood and prepare all the sections to be assembled later at the site. This building was made so it could be taken down in two days and moved to another place after Emanuel Church had built its permanent building.

My missionary colleague, Rich Donaldson, and I worked together on the building, with church people helping. We had only enough money to purchase the materials, so we did all the work ourselves. We assembled the roof trestles first, then went to work on the wall sections, building a frame and nailing corrugated tin to it. The windows were made of one tin sheet, hinged at the top, so we could open them by swinging them up and placing in a stick to hold the window open. All this was transported section by section on a boat trailer to the new lot for Emanuel Baptist Church. There we placed long-lasting hardwood posts in the ground. We then bolted each framed section between these posts with two bolts at the top and two at the bottom. We could take the bottom bolts out and swing the sections up to form an extended roof for overflow crowds. The portable tabernacle could seat more than 200.

As we watched the formation of the portable tabernacle, we often thought of Mark 12:11: *"This was the Lord's doing, and it is marvelous in our eyes."* We praised God for supplying all the materials through the Mitchell Square Baptist Church, in Ontario. Church members worked three nights a week clearing the land with machetes by the light of gasoline pressure lamps, as there were no electric lights installed.

We erected the portable tabernacle in three days, roof and all, much to the astonishment of the neighbors. The tabernacle was taken down a few years later, and the material used in the church's new building that seats nearly 1,000.

CHAPTER 12

Bellavista and Back to Canada

All was functioning well at Emanuel Baptist Church, so the time came for us to move on to a ministry at Bellavista (bay-yaw-veesta, meaning "lovely view") on the shores of the Nanay River on the outskirts of Iquitos. Bill and Ruth Large started this work. Under their direction, a building was erected and regular services held. We took over their work when the Larges went on furlough. We held services on Sunday, Wednesday, and Saturday. Sunday school started at 7:00 a.m. so people could fish or hunt afterwards, a necessity for those who lived off what they caught in the river or in the jungle.

The end of September 1965 was Ruth's last Sunday at Emanuel before joining me in Bellavista. She found it hard to leave Emanuel, as she had important roles at that church, and our children loved it there. Ruth said, "When the Lord says move, it is time to move. There is much work to be done." She soon had the same roles at Bellavista as she had at Emanuel. As if to confirm her move to Bellavista, two people were saved on Ruth's first Sunday there.

Along with taking part in spiritual births, Ruth gave birth to our final child. At noon on October 5, Ruth's labor pains began in earnest. I rushed out to find a taxi to take her to the clinic. None were available, so we took a crowded city bus. Ruth had to stand for the 10 minutes it took to get there. At 2:00 p.m., Cynthia Marie (Cindy) Greenslade was born in the Clínica Stahl in Iquitos. Cindy's birth was the only one of all our children where I was present. When the other children saw her the day after she was born, they were sure the nurse had brought in a Peruvian baby instead of ours because her head was covered with long, thick black hair. Her brothers used to tease her that she was adopted.

The group at Bellavista was made up of about 80 believers, including children. The most active man in the work was Ramón Manihuari. We talked to him about becoming the official leader. After our discussion, he packed his duffel bag and headed out to the bush to escape the responsibility of leadership, which he felt he couldn't do. While out in the jungle, Ramón was bitten by a poisonous snake and had to return to Bellavista for treatment. He told us, "God taught me a good lesson. You cannot run from Him."

Although up to this time, missionaries had always led the services and preached, Ruth began getting Ramón to lead choruses and hymns. She slowly increased his amount of leading until he was doing all the services. I put him in charge of Sunday school. The idea was to give him increasing responsibilities until he was doing the work of a pastor. This new challenge scared him. Later, he told us he went home and considered running to the bush again. However, the snakebite was still vivid in his memory. He reflected on how he had been a sergeant in the army in charge of 200 men. He thought, *I did that, so I could lead 80 people in the services.* He accepted the responsibility, rapidly growing in capability and pastoral know-how. Since that time, he has established two other churches.

By February 1966, the men of the Bellavista church were hard at work, tearing down the old building to put up a new one with a tin roof. The leaf roof of the old building leaked a lot when it rained, and there was always the danger of fire destroying the building. The new church was larger, with wooden walls and floor.

In August 1966, we left for Canada on our second furlough. Before leaving, we had to obtain Cindy's Peruvian passport. Betty and Cindy, born in Peru, had to travel in and out of that country on Peruvian passports. We made reservations to fly on a propeller plane, as the fare was cheaper. When that flight was cancelled, the company flew us to Miami on a jet at no extra cost, and the flight lasted only five hours instead of the usual nine. On arriving in Miami, we found our flight north was cancelled because of a strike. We decided to use the airfare money to buy a car. I purchased a 1959 Chevrolet station wagon that was in excellent condition. We never ceased to be amazed at God's provision of our needs.

On the drive north, we took our time, driving only 250 miles (402 km) a day for two reasons. First, it took a few days to get used to the fast traffic after living for four years in the jungle. Second, the slow pace gave us time to readjust to the North American culture. Three days into the trip, we stopped at a restaurant that offered chicken cooked 14 different ways. I told our children they could choose whatever they wanted. We started with Tom and went down by age, ending with Cindy, who asked for beans and rice.

Furloughs were always a time of walking by faith. We didn't have extra funds to set up housekeeping in Canada. There was always the concern of where we would live and where we would find the furniture and clothes needed to outfit ourselves for the northern winter months. Ruth's parents were a big help in finding a house and outfitting it with furniture, some of which they kept in their basement from the previous furlough; the rest was donated by various people. Missionary cupboards in different churches helped outfit the whole family. Central Baptist Church, in Brantford, made sure we didn't lack in any way. We were able to visit our families and supporting churches each furlough, which meant traveling around 55,000 miles (88,512 km). We enjoyed all of it and had our faith strengthened.

We arrived back in Iquitos from furlough on November 1, 1967. The very next week I held a two-week evangelistic campaign at Calvary Baptist Church in Iquitos. During the first week, the focus of my messages was for believers. The following week was dedicated to reaching the unsaved. In the first few days, four Peruvians trusted in Christ for salvation. We felt great resistance to the message from Wednesday through Saturday. Then on the final evening, the much-prayed-for spiritual fruit came when 17 people manifested their desire to turn to Christ. Five of these were the wives of men who had been saved previously.

We rested for a week after that campaign, then launched another in a new work sponsored by the Bethel Baptist Church in a section of Iquitos called San Antonio (St. Anthony). Missionary Don Bond brought a small generator and showed Bible story slides while Ruth and other missionaries supplied music and stories for the children. The borrowed building we used was crowded each night. Many in the neighborhood heard the gospel over the public address system. Twenty-two people made professions of faith in five nights. Two of them were men who had been sending their children to Bible club all year. Each night they stood outside in the shadows, intoxicated. Toward the end of the campaign they came inside drunk, listened to the message, and trusted Christ as their Savior. From then on they became faithful believers, attending all the services in the new church, and always sober.

We praised God for answering the prayers of those who supported us in our homeland. Between November 1967 and January 1968, there were 44 professions of faith, several families were united in Christ, many believers restored and revived, and several young people were preparing to enter Bible college. We praised the Lord for awakening Christians, especially their interest in establishing new churches. Emanuel Baptist Church had two church plants. Calvary Baptist had a new mission work called Bethany Baptist, and Belén Templo founded a new work called Belén Port Baptist Church.

On March 17, 1968, Ruth and I left the Bellavista church in

Ramón Manihuari's capable hands; we transferred to Calvary Baptist Church because Jerry Russell was soon to go on furlough. He started and built up this work, so we had a strong base with which to work. Several people came to know the Savior right away. A crisis in the family brought salvation to Dario, a man for whom many in the church had prayed for years. His wife, Carmen, was a faithful Christian.

Dario and Carmen's married son, Vincente, was not among those who responded to the gospel. One Sunday evening, after an evangelistic message and singing several verses of an invitation hymn, Vincente chose not to respond to the invitation to come forward and receive Christ as Savior. He said to his mother later, "If they had sung one more verse of the hymn I would have stepped forward." One week later, Vincente was burned badly in a riverboat explosion and died within a few days. His body could not be brought back to Iquitos, so we held a memorial service at the church one Sunday night. Many of his unsaved relatives and friends attended. Jerry Russell preached, and Vincente's father, Dario, accepted the Lord as Savior.

Three months after Vincente's death, his wife gave birth to a baby boy who died at only three days old. Friends from Calvary Baptist Church took the family and the baby to a cemetery on the outskirts of the city. We borrowed a shovel from the French Canadian priests who lived nearby and took turns digging the baby's grave.

During Vincente's memorial service, three young people rededicated their lives to the Lord. We changed the time for the young people's meeting, which resulted in better attendance. Ruth also formed a choir and worked with a male quartet, and various duets and trios. The man who sang bass in the quartet had a great voice. He stuttered badly when he spoke but sang beautifully. Ruth worked with this man by having him sing in duets, trios, and a quartet. After a few months, he no longer stuttered; he later became a pastor.

While we were helping our "spiritual children" grow in the Lord, at the same time we were concerned for the six children God had blessed us with. Educating their children is always a major concern for missionary parents. Our boys were getting to the age where their education could no longer be handled in Peru. Boarding schools can be quite expensive, but God led us to one that was reasonable in price and high in academic standards. We needed such a school so we could stay in the work God called us to do. We learned about Cono Christian School, in Walker, Iowa, because fellow missionary Ernie Olson's children went there.

The boys entered the school in August 1968 and adjusted rapidly, although they complained about the cold Iowa winters. We were able to call them once a week via ham radio, which helped bridge the separation.

We were also encouraged by the growth at Calvary. During 1969, Sunday school attendance increased by 75 percent. In April 1969, we helped Calvary Baptist become an organized church with 45 members. Rodolfo Garcia, a graduate of the Iquitos Baptist Bible Institute, was called as assistant pastor. I worked with the men of the church closing in the property with a wall and finishing the Sunday school building, which had been open on one side. Stray horses often wandered in.

In September, we had our first "mortgage burning" ceremony at Calvary Baptist. The church was debt free, and we looked forward to building the main auditorium. There was no place from which to borrow money, so the plan was to build as money was donated. But lack of funds—among other obstacles—meant the auditorium was never built.

In the latter part of April 1969, Ruth began experiencing severe stomach pains. X-rays showed a bright, shiny lump in her stomach. The doctor in Iquitos called me in and said, "I didn't say anything to your wife as I didn't want to scare her, but I want to scare you. If she was my wife, I would take her out of here today and have her checked to make sure she doesn't have cancer." I made rapid plans for Ruth, Cindy, and me to fly to Miami, Florida, on a flight leaving in two days. Jerry Russell—via ham radio—made an appointment for Ruth with a doctor in Miami, who reserved a hospital bed "just in case." We left the three older girls in Iquitos with their schoolteachers, Sandra Lyons, Fran Weddle, and Muriel Waite. The boys were in boarding school. On May 8, 1969, we arrived in Florida. Ruth was admitted to the hospital the next day for a battery of tests.

While Ruth was in the hospital, I spent my mornings on the beach with Cindy, thinking and praying. For weeks the missionaries in Iquitos had told me I needed to get away to rest. I didn't think so. On that beach, I understood why we were in Miami. I did need a change and a rest. There is always an urgency about missionary work. Much needs to be done, and usually there are not enough people to take care of everything. My responsibilities included field council treasurer, administrator of the mission guest house, co-administrator of the Hills of Zion camp, teaching six hours each week at the Bible institute, maintaining radio contact and arranging supplies for the missionaries on the river, and preparing the paperwork involved in fulfilling government regulations for mission properties. It was too much work, and I was close to nervous collapse. This forced rest was a gift from God.

After five days of tests, Ruth's doctor concluded she did not have cancer. He also thought that probably she had been born with the shiny spot on her stomach. The pain was from damage to the lining of her stomach, probably caused by the spicy foods we ate in Iquitos. He put her on a restricted diet: no spices, no leafy salads, no fruit with seeds—all of which she loved to eat. Ruth asked him how long she had to stay on the restricted diet. He answered, "My dear, with a stomach like yours, the rest of your life." He prescribed medication and recommended that we stay in North America for a couple of months.

Ruth and I decided to spend that recuperation time in

100 FROM THE PRAIRIES TO PERU — AND BEYOND

Canada. Sandra Lyons and Fran Weddle brought the three girls up from Iquitos to be with us. They traveled on the "monkey plane," so nicknamed because it carries only 12 passengers, with the rest of the space taken up with crates of animals and tropical fish. During the girls' flight to join us, an armadillo escaped from its cage and ran loose among the passengers.

Friends in Florida loaned us a car which we used to pick up the boys at their boarding school in Iowa. The whole family was together for the summer, staying with Ruth's parents in Brantford.

In August, we loaded up the family and drove the boys back to the Cono Christian School. Leaving them there and driving to Miami was a heart-searching experience. Ruth and I wondered, *Were we doing the right thing?* Then I remembered an Old Testament verse, Numbers 32:6: *"And Moses said to the children of Gad and to the children of Reuben: Shall your brethren go to war while you sit here?"* Their answer (in 32:16–17) states they would leave their little ones in fortified cities and go to war with their brethren. I realized that the Cono Christian School was our fortified city, with high Christian standards and people called of God to take care of our children. Peace came, and we went on to Peru to resume the spiritual battle on the Amazon.

CHAPTER 13

T.E.E. and Peru's Most Wanted

With church planting expanding, we missionaries became concerned about the lack of pastors for the groups of believers on the rivers. Not enough men graduated from the Bible institute to fill the empty pulpits. We didn't know how to handle this problem.

While we were on furlough, we attended the 150th anniversary of Boston Baptist Church, near Brantford, Ontario. Someone read the history of the church, pointing out that during the first 40 years of its existence, the church had only two pastors—both were farmers who supported themselves. During those 40 years, those two men led in establishing eight more churches in the Brantford area.

Listening to this report, I saw the key to our lack of pastors on the Amazon. We were thinking in today's North American model, where men have to be trained in resident Bible schools before becoming pastors. We needed to think as people did in the pioneer days of North America, where pastors were chosen from the group of believers. On the Amazon, a man in every group led and ministered in a pastoral role but was just called "our leader."

Leaders of the many new groups of believers in Iquitos and on the rivers were asking for training to help them take better care of their congregations. With family and church responsibilities, the pastors couldn't leave their villages to attend the Bible institute. They needed a way to be able to study while continuing their responsibilities.

When we returned to the Amazon, I shared what I had learned at Boston Baptist Church with the missionaries and the pastors. ABWE missionaries and trained pastors began holding short-term training sessions in the towns and villages along the river. We also encouraged leaders to take the Bible institute courses offered by radio. This helped develop their leadership skills, but more was needed. Then we heard of a successful training program in Central America and Bolivia called Theological Education by Extension (T.E.E.). In December 1969, Jerry Russell and I went to Bolivia to investigate extension programs and to search out self-teaching courses.

At that same time, I was named acting director of the Iquitos Baptist Bible Institute in place of Bill Large, who left for a one-year furlough. Our family moved into the upstairs residence at the institute. The field council also voted to initiate an extension department and appointed me as supervisor, with the responsibility of spreading this program wherever it was needed.

The extension program allowed us to take the institute to the leaders, using self-teaching courses and setting up training centers close to where they lived. The self-teaching courses were designed so church leaders could study on their own. Self-teaching courses differ from correspondence courses, which usually have to be sent away to be marked. In the self-teaching courses, material is presented in smaller segments. Students study the sections, answer the questions, and look for the correct answers at the bottom of the page, so they can immediately correct or confirm their work. The lesson books serve as the professors. An essential component, however, is regular visits by a missionary or trained pastor to give a quiz, discuss the material, explain what students didn't understand, and encourage the student/leaders in their ministries. Church leaders generally don't have time to take more than two courses each year. Finishing these courses and the length of time required to graduate are not major issues. Men already in the ministry are more concerned about having something new to preach and teach each week.

The field council divided Peru into two zones, the coast and the jungle, each with a director. The zone was subdivided into geographic areas with a dean over each area. The dean was responsible for overseeing the program and making it possible for all leaders to study.

We started with three levels of study. The first offered a certificate—upon completion of the material—for those who had up to four years of elementary schooling. Many leaders were at this standard or lower. The next level gave a diploma for those who already had five to eight years of schooling. The highest was a bachelor level for those who had completed high school. For them, we added extra reading assignments and papers to write. The first year of the T.E.E. program, one-third of the students were in this level. One university student stated he had never taken harder courses than those offered in the extension program.

The highest level of the T.E.E. program was on the standard of a Bible college. In some ways it was superior, since students learned as they served and practiced while they studied. The students wanted to use what they learned, so it was easy to teach them. Most often the students were mature, already married with a family, and respected leaders in their churches.

In the midst of my organizing the extension department, Tom and David arrived, thanks to supporters who gave funds for our boys to fly down from Iowa. Two weeks later, the plane on which they had flown from Lima crashed, killing 99 people. During the boys' visit, an earthquake struck Iquitos. The three-minute-long quake shook the institute building, making us feel seasick. It also cracked the wall of the parsonage at Calvary Baptist Church.

Shortly after Tom and David arrived, all eight of us left on a rainy night for a river trip with ABWE missionaries Don and Vivian Bond, and Chuck and Carrie Porter and their children. We traveled all night in the ABEM launch with a boat called an *albarenga* tied to the side. We arrived in Nauta the next afternoon. We visited our friends, and the children swam in the creek and fished off the front of the boats. In a short time they caught 20 fish. We held a service in the Nauta church in the evening, slept in the boat, and left at 5:00 a.m. to travel up the Ucayali River, stopping at Bagazán and Jenaro Herrera, where ABWE missionaries Rich and Dee Donaldson had recently begun work.

The next day we arrived in Requena, another 100 miles (161 km) upriver, where Edna Hull worked. The floodwaters had just abated, so there was mud everywhere. When we held a service in the church building in the evening, the benches we sat on sank into the flood-softened dirt floor. First one, then another bench sank and had to be pulled out and shifted to another spot.

After the service we traveled all night to the village of Shebonal, where eight people were baptized in the river with fish jumping out of the water all around them. During the morning church service, hens cackled and roosters crowed so loudly in the house that we could hardly hear the preacher. After the service we left for the village of San Roque, another 100 miles upriver. In various villages, we picked up delegates for an upcoming three-day convention of churches. By the time we arrived for the opening service, 16 North Americans and 43 Peruvians were on board. Our boys put up a tent on the roof of the *albarenga* and slept there.

The convention was the first one held in that area. During the evening service the rain fell so hard on the tin roof that we couldn't hear the preacher. Everything was flooded. We had to take our shoes and socks off and walk through knee-deep water across a long, slippery log over a creek. The women tried to hold a plastic tablecloth over their heads to protect themselves from the pouring rain, with flashlights in their hands, while balancing on the slippery log. Everyone took a turn falling. For the next three days, we had to cross that log every time we went to a service and to eat. One time Ruth's foot sank in the mud above her ankle and she couldn't get it out until I rescued her. All our clothes were muddy, and all washing had to be done—by hand—in the river. The launch roof leaked in several places each time it rained, so we had to quickly find something to cover our suitcases. Every day the boys kept busy putting our mattresses, quilts, and mosquito nets on the roof of the boat to dry.

Two people from San Roque were baptized in the river. After all the rain, the temperature plummeted to 70°F (22°C). Adding the wind chill made us feel the cold even more. We bundled up in everything we could find and we still couldn't get warm. After three days in San Roque, we started back to Iquitos, going as far as the village of Flor de Punga to hold a three-day evangelistic campaign there.

Following these meetings, we returned to Iquitos. Because of the extra passengers and freight heading downriver, some rode in the *albarenga*. This older boat, which needed maintenance, had a rotting, weak hull. Don Bond planned on putting in new planks when we arrived back in Iquitos. When the diesel motor in the ABEM broke a piston, Don and the motor boy shut down the launch and put a 20 hp motor on the *albarenga*. That made it possible to move downstream at a slow pace, but with only one motor for two boats, steering the two vessels was difficult, to say the least. On rivers in the Amazon, trees often float downstream. We tried to avoid hitting them because they can damage the propeller and even the hull. The *albarenga* scraped across some branches of a tree we couldn't miss. We checked inside the hull for damage. It appeared there was none, as no water was coming in. So we went on our way for three more days and nights to Iquitos. Once in port, the motor boy began the post-trip cleanup of both vessels. He found a branch had punctured one of the weaker planks in the *albarenga* and broke off, leaving a piece of wood that snugly plugged the hole. If the branch had not broken off, it would have ripped open a larger hole and sunk the boat. Again we saw God's hand of protection.

Ruth picks up the account:

On the ABEM, I cooked all the meals on a two-burner kerosene tabletop stove. At times I augmented this with another one-burner stove called a primus. On some trips we had up to 50 people on board to feed.

One day as we traveled downstream, I was cooking a meal on our two-burner stove when we ran into a school of fish swimming just under the surface of the water. The approach of the launch agitated them, and a fish one foot (17 cm) long jumped through the front door of the launch, slithered along the floor, and stopped at my feet. I killed, cleaned, and cut it up, then put it in the frying pan, still twitching. God supplied us with the extra fish we needed to complete our meal.

All too soon it was August and Ivor left for Miami with Tom and David, and now Kathy, too, for high school at the Cono Christian School. It got harder each time to see the children go. We didn't expect to see them for two years. Kathy was brave about it and did not cry until I did. The house seemed so quiet with the older children gone, especially at mealtimes. I couldn't let myself think about it. Ivor traveled with them as far as Miami, but he couldn't afford the fare to go with them to Iowa. He said later that saying goodbye to his boys and especially to his little girl, Kathy, was the hardest thing he ever had to do. The children flew to Chicago, where Hube and Elene Watson (from Claim Street Baptist Church in Aurora, Illinois) met them and took them to their home for a few days.

The boys already had winter clothing but Kathy didn't. We wondered how we could afford to buy all the things the three of them needed. Before they left, Ivor gave Kathy $60—all the money he had—so she could buy a winter coat. Three days later on the eve of his return to Peru, he called them on the phone. He asked Kathy if she had bought a coat. Her answer was, "Oh, I have lots of them." Members of the Priquilla Sunday school class in Claim Street Baptist Church gave her three winter coats. Kathy told her dad the kids bought a cassette tape recorder with the $60 so they could send messages back and forth to us. Kathy quickly adjusted to Cono and was soon enjoying school along with the boys. A Women's Missionary Society in North Park Baptist Church in Michigan asked if they could "adopt" Kathy and supply her school needs. This was far above what we could ever ask for. The Lord—and His people—are good.

Big changes in Peru began in 1970. The military government introduced new laws and regulations affecting foreigners and the ministries in which they were involved. The Bible institute board had always been comprised of ABWE Field Council members because the school was owned and operated by missionaries. New laws mandated we organize the institute with its own constitution, statutes, and board, with over 50 percent of the board being Peruvians. Local believers had years of experience on the faculty, but none at board level. Field council members corresponded with Harold T. Commons, president of ABWE, who gave helpful suggestions. We began the process to make sure the Bible institute would be able to continue to function under the new laws. Particular emphasis was given to the extension department. In 1970 there were 19 church leaders taking the extension courses. In the final semester I had to take on a 12-hour teaching load because of the sickness of two professors. I tried the extension method of teaching in the residence classes and found the students liked this way of studying.

In addition to my work at the institute, I continued my work at Calvary Baptist. My aim was to hand over the church to a national pastor. I resigned in December, and the church called Armando Torres as pastor. I no longer attended Calvary but kept active in an itinerant ministry.

One year later I came to realize this was a mistake. Armando Torres told me he thought I had abandoned him. From this experience I realized church-founding missionaries should slowly phase out, giving time for church members to adjust and give their full allegiance to the national pastor. We came up with the saying "Old missionaries shouldn't leave suddenly. They should slowly fade away."

In December 1970, members from Calvary Baptist Church presented a Christmas program at the Iquitos jail. The director of the jail was so impressed that he asked us to continue holding services. We met every Sunday morning, with up to 250 prisoners attending. Jerry Russell taught a five-week course on the gospel of John. Services were held in an open area with the men— including five murderers—sitting on benches. They listened attentively and participated in the singing. After four months of presenting the gospel, we gave the first public invitation. Sixty men responded without hesitation.

In the overcrowded jail, all the prisoners stayed in a common area full of workstands during the day. Many prisoners supported their families by making and selling furniture, so there were a lot of tools available. One prisoner was the most wanted man in Peru for having killed two policemen. An artist's sketch of him was distributed throughout Peru, and he was caught just before escaping to Brazil. On arrival in the Iquitos jail, he made a stiletto out of a file, which he hid in the high rubber boots he wore. He sat at the back, as far as possible from us. The third Sunday he attended, he sprang up and came thumping towards us, stepping over the benches and pushing men out of his way. He didn't bother using the aisle. The guards started moving in, thinking he was going to attack me. When he arrived at the front, he put out his hand and said, "That is what I need! I need Jesus." He received salvation that morning.

He gave his stiletto to the guards and his hostile attitude changed to one of kindness. He made a hand-carved, velvet-lined jewelry box for Ruth in appreciation for his new life in Christ. Two years later, he faced a firing squad, ending his earthly life. But we know that one day we will see him in heaven.

CHAPTER 14

25 Years and Still Going Strong

In 1931, independent missionaries Bill and Elva Scherer began working in the Amazon region of Peru. Their joining the mission in 1939 expanded its territory from the Pacific to Peru and anticipated the opening of other countries. Moving into Peru also necessitated a name change from the Association of Baptists for Evangelism in the Orient (ABEO) to the Association of Baptists for World Evangelism (ABWE).

By 1946, the churches they helped to start banded together to form La Asociación de Bautistas de la Selva (The Association of Baptist Churches of the Jungle). Now, 25 years later, there was a sense of optimism in the work of God in this part of the world.

The ABWE Amazon missionaries felt the need for fellowship and an exchange of ideas with other ABWE South America missionaries. We missionaries organized an All South American ABWE Fields Conference. This was held in March 1971 with ABWE's candidate secretary, Harold Amstutz, and Pastor Floyd Davis, from Colorado, as special speakers. Missionaries came from Colombia, Brazil, and Coastal Peru. Ruth was in charge of planning the meals, buying supplies, and running the dining hall. With help from other missionary women and the Bible institute cook, they fed 45 people for breakfast, 85 at noon, and 30 in the evening for a full week. That same month, Ruth's parents, Harry and Jessie Phillips, came for a visit. Ruth wrote to friends and supporters:

On March 31, we left Iquitos in the launch with Don and
Vivian Bond for a trip up the Ucayali River. This was orientation for us, as we are to take over that ministry while the
Bonds are on furlough. In June we plan to move to the village
of Tamanco where the ABWE floating house is located. Betty
and Karen will stay with ABWE missionaries Dan and Judy
Smith at the Missionary Children's Home in Iquitos. I'll
home-school Cindy in the launch. At first, I was rebellious
about this move to Tamanco because Karen and Betty have to
stay in Iquitos. I couldn't see why the Lord expected me to let
the older kids go to the States and two younger ones also have
to leave home. The Lord had to speak to me, but at last I listened and am looking forward to the move. We will probably
see the girls every other month because of the extension
course program. The kids don't seem to mind. They'll be with
friends their own age.

My parents were with us on the launch. We traveled the
first day until nearly 11:00 p.m., tied up for the night, and left
at 5:30 the next morning. Twenty people were on board plus
one dog, one cat with four tiny kittens, two monkeys, and two
lovebirds. Porpoises jumped in and out of the water all around
us. My father enjoyed steering the boat. In his younger days,
he was a commercial fisherman in Port Dover, Ontario, and
was used to water and boats.

Our first stop was Nauta, where we held a class with two
men studying extension courses. We left early the next morning and ran into heavy rain. The launch was not rain proof, so
we hung up pails here and there and closed the windows. For
supper that night, we ate fish soup, each bowl containing a
whole fish in it (not too appetizing for my parents and a new
ABWE missionary, Darlene Hull, to have fish eyes staring up
at them). Other interesting menus on this trip included monkey meat, tapir, and wild pig. It is almost impossible to buy
beef in the river villages.

Our next stop was Flor de Punga. It was high-water time
on the Ucayali, and everyone—including us—arrived for the

service in canoes. Pastor Mariche had to move upstairs in his two-story house when the bottom floor flooded. He paddled his canoe right in through his front door, tied it up, and climbed up the stairs to the second floor.

Next we arrived in Tamanco, where we stayed during Holy Week. We held special services for four nights, showing slides of the resurrection on an outside wall of the houseboat. So many people came that we divided the services into one for children and one for adults. We also held a wedding and four baptisms. One woman who accepted the Lord brought a chicken to the boat to trade for a Bible, hymnbook, and a chorus book. We encouraged all the new converts to make these purchases, and helped them by trading chickens for the books. We placed the chickens in a coop on top of the *albarenga,* and fed them with corn. For variety from fish, we sometimes ate one. When we returned to Iquitos, we sold the extra chickens to buy more Bibles, hymnbooks, and chorus books to take on the next trip.

My father kept busy fixing the railing around the floating house. He installed another barrel to catch rainwater. My folks swam in the river beside the launch, even though piranhas were swimming all around their feet. My mother washed her clothes in the river while sitting on a balsa raft. We traveled farther up river, stopping in several villages for extension classes.

The last village on our itinerary was Puka Panga, where a Christian man started gospel meetings two weeks before we arrived. He had no experience but was doing all he could and had already led several adults to the Lord. The evening service was rained out, but the villagers were so eager to have a meeting they held it at 8:00 the next morning. Four women and two men accepted the Lord as Savior. We arrived back in Iquitos after a 20-day trip, having traveled 1,000 river miles, (1,609 km).

As supervisor of the extension program, I faced the challenge of how to teach all our church leaders using the T.E.E. courses.

These were men with gifts for pastoral leadership whom God raised up and used to establish new works in many parts of the country. On the Ucayali and Marañón rivers, 45 men wanted to register for the second semester. Using the ABEM launch, we could only regularly visit 15 to 20 students. By the end of 1972 we expected to have more than 60 leaders who wanted to study. Was there a better way of overseeing the extension program?

Yes, by using an airplane. Don Gahagan, a pilot with the South American Indian Mission, was stationed with his floatplane in Pucallpa, 800 miles (1,287 km) upriver from Iquitos. He was ready to take on the job. Our home church supplied the two-way radio we needed to coordinate flights. All we lacked were funds to pay for the cost of flying: $17 per hour at that time. Visits to the students would take 16 hours of flying time, averaging about $7 per student per month. This was good stewardship of time and money when you compared one-way traveling time:

Chanchalaguas (two students) was a three-day jungle walk from Tamanco. It was a three-day journey by launch on two rivers. By plane, the trip lasted only 14 minutes.

To visit the six closest centers downriver from Tamanco took 11 hours by launch, or 22 minutes by plane.

Visiting centers on the Marañón River by launch took 35 hours of travel. The plane could make the trip in one hour and 15 minutes.

I arranged with pilot Don Gahagan to pick me up in Iquitos and fly me up the Ucayali River to visit the extension centers. We completed in three days what had taken 15 days by launch. Three days before leaving we announced our itinerary to the students over the ham radio. They would hear the plane landing and taking off downriver, so they were always in the port waiting for our arrival.

A missionary visit every two weeks was a highlight in the lives of these leaders. It encouraged them and made them realize they were not forgotten. They also could discuss their questions and receive counseling as needed on a more frequent basis.

During the year that Ruth and I filled in for the Bonds on the Ucayali River, we visited various pastors and leaders of different groups. One of them was Ruperto Fuchs, who used to be known as the Mexican dance singer. He traveled from town to town singing in dances, wearing a big Mexican hat, and playing his guitar. He was known to have at least six women in different towns. He had children by two of them in the town in which he lived. He told us the story of his conversion.

He used to travel in a boat on the Ucayali River as a traveling salesman. He bartered items for produce, which he then sold in the city of Pucallpa. He was a heavy drinker and involved in politics. In the dances, he used to shout, "I don't love a woman; I love the women."

In one town when he was drunk, he saw a missionary preaching. In order to make fun of him, he staggered up and asked for the biggest Bible he had. The missionary sold him a large-letter Bible. Ruperto laughed and staggered down to his boat, putting the Bible in the wooden chest where he kept his valuable things. Some months later Ruperto became ill and, after an operation, thought he was going to die. He had not been able to sleep for three days and nights because of excruciating pain. As he lay on his bed, he reflected on what he had heard in the preaching about heaven and hell. He called his common-law wife and told her to bring the Bible from his wooden box. He laid it on his chest and prayed: "I know in this Book it tells how to go to heaven and keep from going to hell. I want to go to heaven, so whatever it takes, do that to me now."

Immediately after his prayer, Ruperto went to sleep. In the morning he woke up and asked for a drink of *chapu,* which is made from crushed ripe plantain. He drank a glass of this and immediately went back to sleep. People in that region believe that if someone is sick and sleeps through the night, wakes up and asks for something to eat, and then goes back to sleep, he is certainly going to die. Villagers began making Ruperto's coffin. After a few more hours' sleep, he woke up and began reading the Bible that had been laying on his chest. Ruperto didn't die. He began getting better and continued to read his Bible. Through reading, he came to the realization that hard liquor is not a good thing. He owned a small store in which he had a number of bottles of Peruvian liquor called *pisco*. He told his woman to take it all down to the river and throw it in, which she did.

Because Ruperto was reading the Bible, townspeople began saying, "He's going crazy." When he had the liquor thrown in the river, they were convinced. Having received Christ as Savior, Ruperto promised the Lord he would make a boat and travel the Ucayali River for one year, telling what Christ had done in his life. He contracted with a commercial house in the city of Pucallpa to sell plastic products in order to support himself. He purchased Bibles and Christian literature at a Christian bookstore in Pucallpa. He built the boat and began traveling, testifying of what Christ had done in his life. He didn't plan on preaching, but this changed one day when he pulled into a town where he had been notorious for his dancing, singing, and political activity. The municipal agent in town asked him to preach to the people. Ruperto answered, "There's no place to preach." The municipal agent said, "You can use the schoolhouse." Then Ruperto said, "I don't have a lamp." The agent said, "I'll supply the lamp." Ruperto had no more excuses for not preaching. He went back to his boat and began praying and crying to God, asking, "What shall I preach?" God's guidance that night led Ruperto into many years of preaching.

When his promised year on the Ucayali River was over, Ruperto returned to the town of Pedrera and married the woman he had been living with. He began preaching there and, with the help of some of the men in the village, built a church that would seat 100 people. We visited him in Pedrera to suggest he enroll in the T.E.E. courses. I heard Ruperto preach that night, all the way from Genesis to Revelation and back again. We put him on the homiletics self-teaching course. By this time he had a good number of converts and an attendance of somewhere around 100 in the church.

We visited him about every three weeks to quiz him on the lessons he had finished and to discuss any questions he had. At first he scored only about 30 or 40 on each quiz, but soon his marks picked up considerably.

On one of my visits two months after he started the course, Ruperto said seriously, "You don't know what you did to me by starting me on this extension course." After supper, he kept me in his house rather than taking me over to the church before the service, which was his custom. I could hear people gathering, and thought it rather strange that Ruperto didn't go over to welcome them. But he had a surprise for me. When he finally said, "It is time to go," we went in the back door of the church and up on the platform. The building was full, with over 100 more on the outside! Ruperto turned to me and said, "See what you have done? You have put an enormous load on my shoulders." Then he laughed and said, "More people come to hear me now because I'm a student." He had become a more important person, someone worth listening to. This was even more apparent when we began visiting him by plane. I learned that the pastors were raised enormously in the eyes of their people, who thought, *He must be very important to be visited by someone in an airplane.*

After four months, I gave Ruperto his final exam, orally, because he was the only student in the center. At that time, we had about 200 students throughout Peru. Quite a number of them had finished the homiletics course, including university students and graduates. I soon realized, as Ruperto answered the questions, that he was going to make a higher mark than anyone else. I began making the questions more difficult and complicated. He would think each question over before answering. He passed with a 95 percent. I told Ruperto that he had the highest mark in all of Peru and asked him how he did it. He replied, "I taught this course every week in Sunday school, in the Sunday morning service, the Sunday evening service, the Wednesday evening prayer meeting, and Friday evening Bible study." He challenged me to ask the people any of the questions I had asked him. "They will be able to answer them," he said. He was right. Ruperto not only had learned the material well, he also had taught it well to his people. I told him I wouldn't preach that night because I wanted to observe him.

Ruperto's style was unique. He walked up and down the aisle of the church, gave a little information, then started popping questions. If someone didn't have the answer, he would say, "You were sleeping," and move on. This kept the people alert, and they learned the material. Ruperto led the men of his church to reach out and establish other churches along the river.

One day, the Roman Catholic priest visited him because he had heard about Ruperto's work. The priest asked several questions and wanted to know how it was that Ruperto knew so much more than he did. Ruperto pointed to the books on his shelf. We supplied all the pastors on the Ucayali River with reference books in Spanish, including the *Jamieson Faucett and Brown Commentary, Haley's Bible Handbook,* a concordance, a full set of books written by Warren Wiersbe, and books by other authors. Ruperto said, "I read and study the Bible and those books. That is where my knowledge comes from."

When I first met Ruperto, his wife wasn't a Christian. She kept a number of Roman Catholic statues in her home. Ruperto told her she had to burn the statues. To avoid this, she asked her next-door neighbor to hide them in her strongbox. (Most families on rivers in the Amazon region own a locked strongbox.) A couple of months after we started visiting Ruperto, we took the neighbor's husband upriver with us in our launch to fish in a small river. We never charged the people we ferried; instead, we asked them to buy a Christian book. These books were written

The first service in our front room in Buenos Aires, Argentina

A visitation team made up of our ABWE missionary families and students from the Word of Life Bible Institute

Ivor baptizes a new believer in Argentina, 1980

A service at Missionary Baptist Church of Bernal, where we worked with Rev. Ismael Cajal

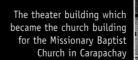

The theater building which became the church building for the Missionary Baptist Church in Carapachay

Ruth and Ivor with Georgi Vins

Preaching in the Soviet Union with the aid of interpreter Mary Smallenberger

Ivor preaching at a service in Ukraine, with the room filled to capacity and people standing outside

Shepherd and sheep on
a road in Romania

Ruth delivering flannelgraph
backgrounds made by women of
Emmanuel Baptist Church, in Simcoe,
Ontario, to a Russian pastor

Group in the
forest on the
outskirts of
Odessa

Witnessing in Ukraine

Dr. Jorge and family

Mid-day crowd on a
downtown Buenos
Aires street

In Kiev

specifically to lead people to salvation in Jesus Christ. On the trip
I saw Ruperto's neighbor reading his book. When he returned
home, he went to talk to Ruperto. Both he and his wife became
believers in Christ. Ruperto's wife was also saved. She went to
her neighbor and asked to have her statues so she could dispose
of them, only to learn the neighbor already had done so!

The Association of Baptist Churches of the Jungle wanted
to celebrate God's mighty work in Amazonian Peru through
the national churches and missionary efforts from 1946–1971.
Records show a percentage growth of 35 percent each year from
1965 to 1970. Plans called for a citywide campaign during the
national holidays in July 1971. We tried to rent a large basketball
coliseum for the campaign. Since this was not possible, the
regional committee of the Association changed the thrust of the
campaign to concentrate on the churches.

Our three children at Cono Christian School wanted to be
in Iquitos with us for the citywide campaign. Their fluency in
Spanish meant they could help in the visitation, the services, and
interpreting for the North American college students who were
to take part. David worked on Saturdays and spare hours, and
saved $100 toward his expense. He even found a free ride to
Miami. Kathy arranged a ride as far as South Carolina. The cost
to return from Miami was $375. Supporters sent sufficient
money to pay their fare all the way from Iowa to Peru, and our
high-schoolers arrived in Iquitos the first week in June.

The evangelistic campaign began on July 3, with an evening
service in each of the twelve churches in the Association in
Iquitos. Nineteen college students spent six weeks with us. They,
along with our four older children and the Bible institute students, canvassed the neighborhood around each church with literature and an invitation to attend the service. They formed a
choir that sang at each service. The churches were full with
crowds of people standing on the outside looking through the
large open windows. In response to the invitation to receive

Christ, people streamed up to the front without hesitation, even from the crowds outside. There were between 25 and 80 decisions each night.

This blitz in the 12 churches was followed by five evening services in a large empty warehouse we rented near the center of Iquitos. All the churches transported their benches to the site, so we were able to seat 1,400 people. The place was full each night, with up to 2,000 one evening. People responded readily to the invitation the first four nights. The last evening, no one came forward, although many unsaved were present. We prayed for God to draw people to Himself. He responded with an earthquake that lasted for three minutes. Earthquakes are never strong in the jungle, but this one rattled the roof and shook the lights. At the same time, a military band, marching by, began to play loudly. This combination startled everyone, and unsaved people flocked to the front. During three weeks of services, more than 800 people were saved. Our four oldest children sang in a quartet, counseled with the unsaved, visited in homes each afternoon, participated in both the children's and adults' service, and had a wonderful time.

Ruth writes about part of that summer:

> On the first day of the visitation program, David came home all smiles. He helped one of the Bible institute students lead a family to the Lord. It was a great experience to hear the young people's expressions of joy—while eating their midnight snack—as they told of guiding the unsaved to the Lord.
>
> After the campaign, we left for a trip up the Ucayali River on the ABEM with our family, eight college students, Jerry Russell, and others, making a total of 26 on board. Other college students traveled with Chuck Porter and his family downriver. Everyone helped with the cooking. The college students saw many new sights and ate different foods, such as turtle stew—with the foot of the turtle on their plate.
>
> One day while I was washing the dishes, David went into the motor room to get a dry tea towel. He came running back, his face white. He ran up to the bridge, yelling that water was

coming into the boat. Ivor hurried down and found the water was halfway up the motor. The packing had come out of the propeller shaft, allowing water to pour in. The sump pump was plugged, so it wasn't pumping the water out. We would have sunk in a very short time if David had not discovered the leak. Ivor called for everyone to grab all the available pots, pans, and buckets and start bailing. In a short time, the problem was fixed and the water dipped or pumped out. We know it was the Lord's protecting hand that saved us from sinking that day.

We held services in five towns. On this trip, Tom led his first service and sounded like an old pro by the third. David also led, and Kathy gave Bible lessons. They all gave their testimonies in Spanish. We were grateful to God and to those whom He prompted to help send our children to Peru. In August they returned to school.

The regional committee of the Association of Baptist Churches broadcasted a regular radio program over one of the Iquitos radio stations. Pastor Daniel Tuanama taught the Bible studies on the program. One day he brought me a letter from a Christian man, Jesús Lazaro, who had moved to San Ramón, a village at the mouth of a large lake on the Marañón River. We had difficulty deciphering the letter, but concluded this man had converts who needed to be baptized. Daniel and I, with my family, fired up the ABEM to answer this call.

We traveled 29 hours up the Amazon and the Marañón rivers to San Ramón. As far as we knew, no missionary had visited there previously. Jesús Lazaro met us in the port. He was from the foothills of the Andes Mountains, where he had been converted to Christ. Because he had become an evangelical, his wife left him, taking their five children with her. He traveled down the Marañón, arrived at San Ramón, and liked the village. He stayed and began to witness of his faith in Christ. Before long he had a group of new believers to fellowship with.

Jesús proudly showed us the church they were building.

There were 25 believers in that village and another 25 in Bagazán, across the lake. He had led them all to the Lord. None of the believers had been baptized, including Jesús Lazaro himself. Daniel and I talked with each believer in preparation for a baptismal service. On the first Sunday of our visit, we baptized all 25 in San Ramón and a few from Bagazán.

Jesús could barely read and write, which explains why we had difficulty reading his letter. He also had the highest male voice I have ever heard. When he preached he tilted his head back slightly and the gospel message flowed out, and people listened to him spellbound. Since we first met him, Jesús has established eight churches and completed several T.E.E. courses.

On this trip, Daniel and I held services in five different villages. Over 50 people accepted the Lord as Savior. One man heard the gospel as a child but hadn't heard it since. He had privately accepted the Lord, but now made a public confession of his faith. Soon after our visit, he began holding services in his home. He did not know much about the Bible, but was doing his best. So many people bought Bibles on this trip that we ran out.

Later, we had a profitable two-week visit on the Marañón River. Prior to our trip, a man from Brazil named Señor da Cruz had gone to each village erecting large wooden crosses. Three quarters of the people in each village wore wooden crosses on their necks. Señor da Cruz was neither Roman Catholic nor evangelical; he was teaching a new religion. Many people worshipped him as their god, although some thought his teaching was not true. They asked us questions and were ready to listen to the gospel. We held services in five villages and saw 43 decisions for Christ. We were able to organize two groups with their own national leaders.

My work in the extension department of the Bible institute involved writing courses, typing stencils, proofreading, running off copies, and making up the books. In addition to visiting students in our own area, I also visited the extension centers in other parts of Peru, and went to Colombia to talk with people interested in starting the extension courses there.

When missionary colleagues became ill, Ruth and I left Tamanco to live in Iquitos from February to May. I ministered in the churches, wrote courses, and prepared for furlough. We planned to fly to Miami through Leticia and Bogotá, Colombia, to take advantage of cheaper airfares. That meant we needed exit and re-entry papers in order to leave Peru. When I applied for them at the immigration office in Iquitos, the secretary in charge told me I would have to obtain the papers in Lima. He gave no reason for this.

When our children left for boarding school, Ruth and I promised to do whatever was necessary to attend graduations and weddings. Tom would graduate from Cono Christian School the first week in June. We planned on buying a car in Miami and driving to Iowa. In order to have time to do this, we left Iquitos on May 16 for Lima to complete our paperwork.

We arrived in Lima on Saturday, although government offices didn't open until Monday. Our flight was scheduled to leave the next Friday. My agent assured me four days was ample time, as the exit and re-entry papers were issued within two or three days. Early Monday morning, I went to the Immigration offices, taking Karen with me. We sat watching the office workers arrive. We noticed the secretary in the first office looked angry. A sign indicated that her office was the place I was to present all of our documents. I approached her window with our passports and Peruvian documents in hand. The angry secretary took them and, in a loud voice, said, "I'm going to find something wrong with these documents. You just wait and see." I was confident all was in order, so I didn't worry. She pulled out her files on us and began checking each item. I thought, *She is just doing her job. There should be no problem*. Then she triumphantly announced, "Aha, this girl, Karen, has been in Peru illegally for nine years." The secretary told me we couldn't leave the country until Karen's immigration status was corrected. I asked, "How long will that take?" Her answer was, "At least six weeks. The paperwork has to be done in 12 different offices."

After five years as residents in Peru, we were granted permanent immigration visas.

Karen was born in Canada during our furlough in 1962. We brought her to Peru on a three-month tourist visa and applied to have her placed with the rest of the family as an immigrant. The government official in charge of the immigration office in Iquitos had us fill out the necessary papers, received full payment for his work, and issued Karen a Peruvian immigrant visa. The official assured me all was in order. What I didn't know was that he pocketed the money and filed her application in the wastepaper basket. Four years later, the same man issued all of us re-entry permits, including an illegal one for Karen. We exited and re-entered Peru through Leticia, Colombia, 350 miles (563 km) downriver from Iquitos. The immigration office in Iquitos cleared our paperwork, unbeknownst to the headquarters in Lima. As far as they were concerned, Karen had lived in Peru illegally from 1962 to 1972—through no fault of ours.

A delay of six weeks meant we would not reach Iowa in time for Tom's graduation. I prayed, "Lord, you know about our promise to attend our children's graduations. Now guide me in what I must do." I phoned our tourist agent and asked what I could do to speed things up. He advised me to go to the manager who was in charge of the angry secretary, present the difficulties with Karen's paperwork, and tell him of our desire to arrive in time for our son's graduation.

That's what I did. The manager heard me out, initialed my application to add Karen to our immigration visas, and told me to go on to the next office. In offices two through four, the managers were sympathetic, initialed the papers, and sent me on to the next office. I was thanking God for working in such a wonderful way when the manager in office number five, Mr. Flores, after hearing my oft-repeated story, said, "I don't have anyone to work on your papers. They are all busy. Come back next week." I began to repeat my story. He pointed and said, "There is the door." When a government official in Peru says that, you use the door. If you don't, he can have you arrested. So I used the door. I stood in the hallway, holding Karen's hand, praying, "Lord, you know all about this. I put it in Your hands to work it out."

A year before this incident, Mr. Garcia, from the Immigration Department in Lima, came to Iquitos to investigate the actions of the city's chief of immigration. His investigation resulted in the discharge of that man from his duties. While Mr. Garcia was in Iquitos, he and I became friends. As I finished my prayer, a man dressed in a suit came up the stairs—Mr. Garcia! We greeted each other with the traditional Peruvian hug and chatted a bit about Iquitos and the happenings there. Then he asked me what I was doing in the hallway. I repeated my story, and he asked me how things were going. I told him Mr. Flores had just kicked me out of his office. His response was, "He did? Come with me." As I re-entered the office we had just left, Mr. Garcia told Mr. Flores, "This is my good friend from Iquitos. His paperwork must be done immediately!" Mr. Garcia was Mr. Flores's boss, so Mr. Flores instructed his secretary to begin working on my papers. I needed to go to the immigration photo lab to have Karen's picture taken. I thanked Mr. Garcia and went with Karen to find the lab. When I entered, I saw the photographer place a new 36-frame roll into his camera. He took Karen's picture and told me to return the next day.

I arrived at the lab the next morning at 8:00 a.m., eager to keep the paperwork moving. The photographer protested that he had taken only two pictures on that roll, and I would have to wait till the other 34 were taken. His secretary spoke up: "Mr. Flores called and said 'immediately'." The photographer took his camera off its stand and disappeared into his darkroom. A short while later, he reappeared with the finished picture. Karen and I returned to Mr. Flores' office and, from there, on to the next six offices, where the paperwork was handled right away. The vice-chairman of the department took Karen's papers into the last office to have them signed. He handed them to me at noon on Tuesday. I took them back to the first window to receive the exit and re-entry permits. The look of astonishment on the angry secretary's face was priceless. I thought, *There is nothing more adventurous than serving God. He knows exactly what He is doing!*

We left on Friday, flying into Miami. I bought a car and we drove to Iowa, arriving in time for Tom's graduation.

CHAPTER   15

Family   Focus

Our family spent the summer of 1972 together in Brantford, Ontario, where Tom and David got summer jobs. In August, Tom entered Baptist Bible College, in Clarks Summit, Pennsylvania. David returned to Cono Christian School for his last year of high school, and the four girls went to schools in Brantford.

Ruth and I began visiting our supporting churches. During meetings at the Boston Baptist Church, the church surprised us with $200 for our mission account and $50 for personal spending. We used the personal gift to buy books and school supplies, as well as some groceries. The next time we needed to go grocery shopping, our support check hadn't arrived. Ruth spoke at the Women's Missionary Society meeting at Rawdon Street Baptist Church, in Brantford. The women gave us a food shower and a gift of $20. God supplied our needs day by day through His faithful people.

At the end of September, I spoke at Cedarville College, in Ohio, and at some churches in that state. I called Ruth each evening. In one conversation she told me Tom had phoned her twice, saying he was unhappy at Baptist Bible College. When I called Tom, he said the college, the teachers, and the soccer were terrific, but he had come to the conclusion the school was for preachers. He said, "Dad, I can never be a preacher like you." He felt he was out of God's will and wanted to study to become a professional artist.

I cancelled my last speaking engagement in Ohio and drove
to Clarks Summit. I watched Tom play in a soccer game where
he made two goals. When I complimented him, he responded
that he thought it was stupid to chase a ball around a field. He
had decided to leave college that very week. I invited him to go
along with me to the missionary conference at Colonial Hills
Baptist Church, in Atlanta, Georgia. He helped me drive, and we
talked over many things. On the way, we stopped at Bob Jones
University to investigate the art department. Tom liked what he
saw and later applied and was accepted.

Tom returned to Brantford with me and began looking for a
job. David wrote from Iowa that he badly needed a winter jacket.
A few hours after we read the letter, Ruth received a phone call
from Mrs. Berna Callan of the Women's Missionary Society,
Immanuel Baptist Church, in Milton, Ontario. She asked if the
society could buy a winter jacket or some other clothing for one
of the boys. God answered David's request in a hurry that time.

Our younger children had difficulty adapting to the cold climate. After the first snowfall, we bundled them up for play out-
doors. The only shoes they had were plastic sandals from Peru.
We slipped their sandaled feet inside winter boots and thought
they would have no problem out in the snow. But they got tired
wearing those heavy boots, took them off, and ran around in the
snow in their summer sandals. They had no experience with
snow, and their feet started to freeze. Fortunately, we saw what
they had done and called them inside. We placed their feet in
water to bring the circulation back as fast as possible. There was
a lot of crying as their feet warmed up. The children soon were
excited about the snow and collected two bowls of it, which they
put in the refrigerator.

Tom got a job laying sod at Central Baptist Church, in
Brantford. He came home one day and said, "Can you imagine
laying sod in a snowstorm?" When that job was finished, Tom was

offered a job with a Christian printer in Woodstock, 30 miles (48 km) from Brantford. He had learned the printing trade at Cono Christian School.

In December, Tom complained of pains in his lower abdomen. He told us this had occurred off and on for five years. Four different doctors had checked him over and did not find any cause for his symptoms. We took him to Dr. Young, our family doctor in Brantford, who was sure the problem was Tom's appendix. He referred Tom to a surgical specialist. X-rays showed there was a serious problem, so the specialist scheduled Tom for an exploratory operation.

Tom was admitted to Brantford General Hospital on January 16, 1973, for tests. The specialist gave these possibilities: an intestinal amoebic cyst, a benign tumor, a ruptured appendix, or cancer. The surgeon said he wouldn't know until he operated. If it proved to be cancer, he would have to remove part of Tom's intestine. The operation was successful and revealed Tom's appendix had ruptured and then ulcerated.

Tom soon recuperated and found a job at the White Farm Implement warehouse, in Brantford. As he gathered items from the bins in different aisles, he kept meeting a fellow employee, a student working to earn money to go back to university. Every time they met, he asked Tom a question about the Bible. One day when he and Tom were eating lunch together, the student asked questions and Tom answered them. Suddenly Tom noted the 30 employees in the lunchroom were all listening to him. He realized he was preaching. The thought came to him that he *could* be a preacher. Later in the year, Tom reapplied to Baptist Bible College, the school he left because it was "a preacher's school." Today, Tom is a pastor.

Our family traveled 44,000 miles (70,809 km) visiting supporters, and I made a trip west to Alberta to visit my family. By August 1973, we had our needed support and funds for travel, and we were cleared by the ABWE finance department to return to Peru. I drove Tom and David to Baptist Bible College first, then we drove Kathy and Betty to Cono Christian School for Kathy's last year of high school and Betty's first. Leaving them again was heart wrenching.

Ruth and I, with Karen, and Cindy, drove to Florida at the end of August with 500 pounds (227 kilos) on top of the car. The trunk and half the back seat were also full.

We departed from Miami on September 21, to Bogotá, and Leticia, Colombia, and from there to Iquitos. The leg from Bogotá to Leticia on an old Colombian army plane was a rough flight through a rainstorm. One man's soft drink hit the ceiling. Water ran down the aisle of the plane and out the back door. A suitcase of our clothes didn't make it onto our plane and didn't arrive until a week later. A lot of our clothes got wet. Mildew set in, and even though Ruth washed out everything right away, some clothes had to be thrown out.

We arrived in Iquitos on September 23, the day before Karen and Cindy had to start school. Their classes ran from 7:30 a.m. until 12:45 p.m. each day. This left them free each afternoon when the temperature is unbearably hot. Cindy had forgotten a lot of her Spanish and had trouble getting used to the bugs. The first night she went to take a shower, she found a big spider on the back of the door and six cockroaches on the shower curtain. She let out a scream and ran into our room.

While house hunting, Ruth and I found prices had greatly increased since oil had been discovered up the Tiger River, one of the tributaries of the Marañón. Many oil workers had arrived in Iquitos, which made housing scarce. Once again we stayed in the mission guesthouse.

After quite a search we rented a house for $185 per month. We had only allotted $100 per month for rent, so we had to skimp to make the payments. But the house was brand new, and boasted a small front yard with plants, a big living room, two bedrooms, and a kitchen, all on one side. The other side was a long hallway that looked like a patio with an indoor garden. We moved into the house on November 27, 1973. Half the Greenslade family was back "home" in Peru.

CHAPTER 16

Change in the Air

Ruth starts this account:

On December 28, we set out for the Convention of Baptist Churches meetings in the village of Caballo Cochillo (meaning, little lake). This was a one-hour speedboat ride downriver from Iquitos. We stayed with Duane and Carol Roduner in their launch for a week. Almost everyone in this village was a Christian. Visiting delegates helped the believers at Caballo Cochillo organize their church, then hold a dedication service which included the church's first communion service.

On the evening of December 31, the pastor's 12-year-old boy was bitten on the hand by a poisonous snake. He had been bathing in the river right in the spot where a baptismal service was held that afternoon. His arm was swollen, and he was writhing with pain. The family treated the bite in the traditional way, by holding the boy's hand over a steaming pot, which caused it to blister, making matters worse.

After the New Year's Eve service a delegate from the next village downriver was returning home with his pregnant wife and another man in their canoe at 2:00 a.m. When they reached the middle of the river (one and a half miles or 2.4 km wide at that point), a heavy wind caused high waves. The canoe filled up with water faster than they could bail it out. They yelled for help, and someone heard them. Some of the men still at the convention lined the bank, yelling, "Wait! Help is coming." Duane Roduner got into his speedboat with an-

131

other man and headed out to the rescue, yelling, "Where are you?" The men along the bank guided them by crying out, "Farther downriver." The dark, cloudy night made it hard to distinguish a canoe from the logs and trees floating in the river. Duane's boat passed them twice before he finally found them. The Lord sent a big tree with forked branches right to them. The three in the canoe grabbed on to it and ran the canoe up over the forks, hanging on, yelling for help. By the time Duane got to them, they had floated to the other side of the river, opposite their village.

Ivor returned to Iquitos and attended the New Year's program at Calvary Baptist, ate supper after the midnight service, and played volleyball until 3:30 a.m. He slept three hours, then went to the port at 8:00 a.m. Pastor Ricardo Panduro and his son wanted to return to the convention in time for Ivor's class at 10:00 a.m. Arriving at the boathouse where the speedboat was kept, they found someone had pulled the plug out, so the boat and motor sank. They had to get the boat out, take the motor apart to dry it, get it checked, and finally arrived at the convention at 1:30 p.m. Ricardo and his son got out of the speedboat, rocking it as they did, toppling Ivor over the side. He grabbed the side of the boat as he went down, so he got just his seat and back wet. Everyone on the bank laughed. He went up the bank, ate lunch, and then took the boy with the snakebite to a small hospital in the town of Indiana, about one hour downriver. The boy remained in the hospital and with treatment survived.

During the mid-year school vacation, we participated in a young people's camp at Hills of Zion campgrounds, where 190 young people attended. The men and boys had to sleep in the dining room, the light-generating room, and the chapel, as there were not enough cabins.

On the last night, the campfire finished near midnight because so many young people wanted to give testimonies. The girls went to their cabins and the boys to the various spots where they had found a place to sleep. Just after midnight, the girls in one cabin began to scream. Ivor and some of the young men ran to see what the problem was. There was a poisonous snake in the middle of the cabin floor. They killed that one, then noticed others slithering under the platform where the girls slept. There were large cracks in the dirt floor under the platform where the snakes hid. Ivor crawled under the platform, with a shovel in his hands, to scare the snakes out. Men waited outside the cabin with clubs. Ivor began chopping around the cracks with a shovel. The snakes hurriedly escaped through an open space under the walls, and each one was killed as it appeared outside. There were five snakes in all. Ivor continued chopping the dirt and filling in all the cracks so no more snakes could hide there. The camp caretaker explained that one of the snakes was a female, and the four males were after her!

In looking back over 1975, I found much to rejoice about. People were saved almost every time I preached. Pastors often consulted with me, looking for help in their work, but somehow my ministry in Iquitos seemed like sawdust. I wondered what was the matter. Was I failing in my spiritual life? I was no longer experiencing excitement in God's work.

Dr. Don Jennings, at that time acting as pastor to the ABWE missionaries, arrived in Iquitos to visit all the members of our field council. In tears, I unburdened my heart to him. After I finished, he quietly said, "Brother Ivor, have you ever considered that God might want you to go somewhere else?" I hadn't. Ruth and I answered the call of God and went to the Amazon for life, so leaving to go elsewhere never crossed our minds.

In contemplating the "dryness," however, we realized God might want us to go to some other place. Although we didn't know our future area of ministry, we asked God for direction and kept busy in the work in Iquitos. We knew the Spirit of God leads those who *"minister to the Lord,"* as Barnabas and Saul did in Acts 13:2.

On February 5, 1976, Joy Reid, a close friend of ours from
Huntsville, Ontario, arrived for a one-month visit. We rarely had
visitors on the Amazon, so her time with us was special for Ruth
and me, and for Karen and Cindy. Joy adapted rapidly to the culture of Peru and enjoyed going out on her own. During this
time, Ruth and I were both writing courses for the Bible institute, involved in camp work, and making visits on the river.

ABWE missionaries didn't know how long they would be
allowed to remain in Peru. The government was no longer
renewing resident visas to people from the United States, but
continued to issue them to Canadians, so Ruth and I were not
affected by this crisis.

On September 11, Ruth wrote to Kathy, Tom, and David at
Baptist Bible College:

> Dad hasn't been satisfied here this term and is praying the
> Lord would show us definitely what He wants us to do. He
> wants to prepare extension lessons, print them, supply the stu-
> dents with courses, and visit the extension centers. He can't do
> it here, as he is too involved in other work. We have been in
> the Amazon for so many years that everyone wants him to do
> this and that, leaving no time for the extension courses. He
> thinks these courses are more important now, as the country
> may be closing to us. Even if missionaries aren't in the coun-
> try, the courses will continue to be used. At the last field
> council meeting, we told our fellow missionaries that when
> we go to Canada for furlough, we would not be returning to
> the Amazon. There was dead silence. They were shocked, and
> some cried. Later, Dad told the Peruvian pastors of our deci-
> sion. Some of them cried. It is going to be hard leaving after
> being here for 20 years. If we return to Lima, we will proba-
> bly get back once in a while for ministries on the Amazon.
> Now our problem is figuring out what to sell and what to take
> with us. Our news was a shock to everyone, as Jim and Sharon
> Evans are leaving in November and won't be coming back to

Iquitos. They don't know what they will be doing either, but feel their work here is finished.

Because of our immigrant status and the fact that we are Canadians, we think we should return to some place in Peru, probably Lima because there are good printers and it is easier to send out the courses from there. The only problem is, I suffer asthma attacks much more on the coast of Peru because of the desert dust. We hope this isn't too much of a shock to you. Dad is a different person since he decided about the change. It seems that a whole big load has been lifted.

We began the process of turning our work over to others and preparing for departure in May 1977. Because of Ruth's acute asthma on the coast of Peru, we realized we could not relocate there. We continued waiting for God's guidance. We sold many of our things. We still had the steel barrels with removable tops, in which we originally shipped supplies to Peru. We filled these with books and other items we wanted to keep, placing them in storage until we could ship to wherever we would go.

In 1977, missionaries in São Paulo, Brazil, organized a conference for all the ABWE missionaries in South America. I was to attend as a delegate, and we decided Ruth would go with me in celebration of our 25th wedding anniversary. Karen and Cindy stayed with Fran Weddle. They were not enthused about being left behind, but it was good preparation for future separations.

Eighty ABWE missionaries from South America attended the conference. Ruth and I felt like foreigners when we visited the churches, as they speak Portuguese in Brazil and we speak Spanish. On our return trip we visited missionary friends and did some sightseeing in Asunción, Paraguay, and in Cuzco, Ica, and Lima, in Peru.

During our last month in Iquitos, Ruth and I spent most of our time training future teachers at the Bible institute. The director, Ricardo Panduro, asked me to make sure they understood and believed Baptistic faith and practice. I taught the teachers how to find the basis for their beliefs in the Word of God. I also tried to visit each of the 12 churches in the Association of Churches in Iquitos. I took pictures of each church and the pastor and his wife. We didn't tell the church when we would be visiting; we just showed up. As soon as they saw us at the door, they welcomed us and announced I would preach. I had to go prepared. I tried to visit three churches each Sunday morning, speaking at 8:00, at 9:30, and again at 11:00. At one church they changed the time of the service just so I could preach.

We left Iquitos in May and flew to Scranton, Pennsylvania, in order to attend David's graduation from Baptist Bible College. Ruth's parents drove from Ontario, as a surprise for everyone. Betty, who lived with Don and Vivian Bond, in Binghamton, New York, during her last year at Ross Corners Christian Academy, also attended the celebration.

We moved into a house in Brantford that Ruth's parents and the people of Central Baptist Church furnished for us and began preparing for trips to our supporting churches. I wanted to prepare a presentation of our ministries in Peru using slides stored with Ruth's folks, but I couldn't find them anywhere.

I started reporting to churches the next week, driving to Grand Rapids, Michigan, to speak at North Park Baptist Church. We were in Binghamton, New York, for Betty's high school graduation near the end of June. Then Ruth and I drove to Huntsville, Ontario, to speak at Riverside Baptist Church. We stayed with our friends Joy and Sherwood Reid. She accompanied us back to Brantford the next day. It was lovely to have her with us, but I wondered why she wanted to make that trip.

We found out the next evening. Our children surprised us with a 25th wedding anniversary celebration at Central Baptist Church, where 135 people signed the guest book. The biggest surprise that evening was when I found out where my slides were. Our children had created a special presentation called

"Twenty-five Years Together." They used two slide projectors with voice and music background. Ruth and I watched it with delight and often with tears.

In July, we attended ABWE's annual Missionary Enrichment conference, held that year in Waterloo, Iowa. Jim Evans had recently returned from a survey trip to Buenos Aires, Argentina, with Pastor Dan Gelatt from First Baptist Church, in Elkhart, Indiana, and Bill Hopewell, ABWE administrator for South America. Jim asked me about our plans for the future. I told him we were not sure where God wanted us to go. Jim told me he and Sharon were transferring to Buenos Aires, and asked, "Why don't you come to Argentina with us so we can serve together as a team to open the ABWE work in that country?" I turned him down because I felt Argentina was too far from Canada, making it too costly for our children to visit us. Ruth told me later that she just shivered when Jim asked his question because she already felt we should go to Argentina.

Ruth and I spent a night in October with the Evanses in Cass City, Michigan. Jim told me of the opportunities in Buenos Aires. After awhile, I realized I was suggesting how "we" could do things in that city. Jim sat listening and smiling. At that moment, I knew God wanted us in Argentina.

Later that week, I called Bill Hopewell and told him of our conviction that we should go to Argentina with Jim and Sharon. On April 4, 1978, the ABWE board assigned us to work in Argentina. The front cover of the *Message* magazine announced that ABWE was to enter Argentina. The second paragraph read, "Two experienced missionary couples, Jim and Sharon Evans, and Ivor and Ruth Greenslade, have expressed God's leading to work in Argentina. Both couples have served the Lord as missionaries in Peru."

Jim and I had worked together on many projects in Peru, so we looked forward to this new teamwork challenge. We began planning how we would open the work in Buenos Aires. We knew that in the capital city, two couples and a single woman, graduates of the Word of Life Bible Institute in Argentina, wanted to work with us to learn church planting and pastoral ministry. This meant we could start with a multiple church staff. We began visiting pastors with a multiple church staff to find out how they administered their team. We also attended a seminar in Chicago to learn more about church administration.

Jim and I reached out by faith to grasp the future. We asked God to guide us in establishing ten churches in Buenos Aires and the surrounding area within ten years. While making these plans, Ruth and I continued visiting our supporters, including them in our vision for this new work in Argentina.

We needed visas for Argentina. Joe Jordan, director of Word of Life in Argentina, offered to sponsor us and process our visa applications. We sent him the information in the mail and waited for an answer. We were told the process would take about six weeks.

While waiting, we visited my family and our supporters in Alberta. Returning from that trip, we took Betty for her first year at the London Baptist Seminary, in London, Ontario (now Heritage College, Cambridge, Ontario).

In September, Ruth and I took a one-month course on personal evangelism taught by Rev. Doug Erickson, an associate pastor with Rev. Dan Gelatt. We already were experienced in personal evangelism but wanted all the expertise we could gather. While we took this course, Pastor Gelatt coached me on how he administered and trained his church staff of eight associate pastors.

During our wait for visas, we received a telephone call from our son David, then living in Chile, where he taught at the Santiago Christian Academy. David discovered that the information we sent to Argentina for our visas was lost in the mail. We re-mailed it in two separate registered envelopes and reapplied for our visas. Because of the delay, we decided to pick up our visas in Paraguay.

How did Paraguay enter into this? Bill Hopewell asked us to stop there on our way to Argentina and spend a few weeks with the ABWE missionaries who were having difficulty working out the administration and functioning of their field council. I asked Bill, "What do you want me to do?" His answer was, "Just be there." He thought that the presence of experienced missionaries from a field council that functioned well would help the ABWE missionaries in Paraguay.

We expected to leave from Toronto on October 7 on Eastern Airlines to Peru, to finish business there before going to Paraguay and Argentina. Then I received a call from Russ Ebersole, then ABWE's administrator for the Far East. Russ asked me to fly to the Philippines to speak at a conference for pastors and Bible women. I asked him what I should speak about. Russ replied, "Just tell about your work in Peru. That will be a help to the Christian workers there." I accepted the challenge, so our plans were changed.

We had made arrangements to stay at the D & D Missionary Homes in St. Petersburg, Florida. In those days, missionaries could stay there for a nominal fee of $5.00 a night. Or they could work a certain number of hours helping in the upkeep of the property. Ruth and I, with Karen, Cindy, and our friend Betty Ganton left Brantford on October 12 and flew to Florida.

I left a week later and, after 18 hours flying, landed in the Philippines. ABWE missionary Stan Holman met me and took me to his home where I slept a few hours before flying to Iloilo to speak the next morning at the Doane Baptist Church. Dr. Zamar, president of Doane Baptist Bible Institute, and ABWE missionary Craig Kennedy took me to the institute. A big sign in front of the institute read, "All Asian Evangelism Conference." At the top of the sign was Dr. James Jeremiah's name, and further down, my name. I knew Dr. Jeremiah was the chancellor of Cedarville College, and wondered, *What on earth am I doing here?*

I spoke in two services at Doane Baptist Church, one in

English and one translated into the Ilonggo dialect. In the evening, Doane Baptist Bible Institute held a graduation service for the first five students graduating from their extension program. That excited me because of my involvement in T.E.E. in Peru.

I taught 90-minute classes each morning and afternoon. Although I had sufficient material with me, no one had told me the main emphasis of the conference beforehand. This meant a lot of studying, preparing, and arranging lectures. I got up at 3:30 each morning and worked throughout the day. Pastors and their wives, Bible women, evangelists, and ABWE missionaries—550 in all—attended from all over the Philippines. I was impressed with the quality of leadership of the Association of Churches and at Doane Baptist Bible Institute.

I was able to present various aspects of our work in Peru that were applicable to the Philippines. On the flight out to the Philippines, I worried about my lack of knowledge of Oriental culture. On Monday, as I mixed with the pastors and evangelists, I got the feeling they were much like Peruvians. I even tried a couple of Peruvian jokes and people laughed. Then I remembered the Philippines had been under Spanish rule for 376 years, and was greatly influenced by Spain. The Spanish had settled in Peru, so I found much of Filipino culture just like Peru. I felt at home with the people in the Philippines.

CHAPTER 17

A Step of Faith into the Dark

Ten years before we Greenslades set out for Argentina, two women who were new believers in Christ began praying that God would send someone to establish a Bible-teaching church in the north-side suburb of Buenos Aires, where they lived. As they prayed, the Lord called the Evans and the Greenslade families from Peru to Argentina.

When I returned from the Philippines to St. Petersburg, Florida, on October 8, 1978, I phoned our travel agent, who assured me everything was in order and the tickets for our flight to Peru were at the airport. It was good we went to the airport early. The "promised tickets" did not exist, nor were any reservations booked for us. The ticket agent said they had been lost. In actual fact, the flight was overbooked and a lot of people—including us—were bumped off the flight. After a half-hour wait we were given new tickets in first class.

During the flight, the pilot took Karen and Cindy into the cockpit. The sun rose at 5:30 a.m., just as we passed the highest mountain peak in Ecuador—a beautiful sight. We went through immigration in Peru with a minimum of difficulty, but when we went to the baggage claim area, we discovered two footlockers were missing. They had been left in Miami and wouldn't arrive until the next day. We had to leave that evening for Iquitos so we asked airline personnel to keep the bags under lock and key until our return.

We took care of necessary matters in Iquitos and finalized

legalities in Lima—or so we thought. We flew into Asunción, Paraguay, where Ruth, Karen, Cindy, and I spent three and a half months. Our assignment in Paraguay included helping ABWE missionaries revise their field council constitution and handbook.

But Paraguay was just a stop on our journey to Argentina. In dealing with the Argentine consulate, we learned that the police certificates given to us in Peru were not correct. We tried to have correct ones sent from Peru, but were told we had to return to Peru to have them completely redone. That meant flying back to Peru for two and a half weeks to get this all straightened out. The Lord had His hand in this, as a new ruling just passed in Peru stated that the only way we could terminate our Peruvian visas and have another family replace us was to apply in person. We had to present our Peruvian income tax declarations for the past five years. These were stored in our barrels in Iquitos. In getting the tax forms, I noticed as I moved the barrels that the sealing rings on two of them had broken. I was able to fix them before they were shipped to Buenos Aires.

We flew back to Paraguay to finish our temporary assignment and apply for admission to Argentina. We now had all the necessary papers for our Argentine visas, but the red tape was nowhere near finished. Our birth and marriage certificates had to be translated into Spanish. We needed blood tests, vaccinations, physicals, and X-rays. All of these papers had to be legalized by multiple government offices. By March 15, 1979, this had all been completed

We left Asunción, Paraguay, at 7:00 p.m. that same day by bus, and arrived the next afternoon in Buenos Aires at 3:00 p.m. We unloaded our baggage for inspection at the Argentine border and later at a police checkpoint down the highway. Customs officials went through everything thoroughly. The police were looking for drugs, but didn't open any of our bags. We just unloaded them and loaded them back up again.

Word of Life missionary Joe Jordan and fellow missionary

Jim Evans met us at the bus station in Buenos Aires, settling us into a furnished house owned by furloughing missionaries. This gave us time to look for a house to rent.

At that time, Buenos Aires had a population of just over 12 million people. The city seemed unending. Many main streets had six or eight lanes of traffic, although cars often lined up twelve abreast as drivers used every available space. People look and dress much like North Americans, because most are of European background.

Everything seemed expensive to us by comparison with Peru, including the used furniture we found to furnish our own house. Food and clothing cost more than in Canada! Because of the high inflation and the fact that the government was restricting the devaluation of their money in relation to the U.S. dollar, rent was astronomical. Inflation rose 12 percent each month, but the government allowed the American dollar to increase in value by only 4 percent a month. This meant the exchange rate gave us less and less Argentine money each month. Most rental properties cost from $400 to $1,000 a month.

We wanted to find an area in the city where we could settle and begin our church planting. I traveled around by bus and train looking at different areas to find a place we could afford. Carlos DiLeo, one of the Bible institute graduates who was working and training with us, rented a house in an area called Carapachay. I contacted a real estate agent in that area. We found a house that rented for the equivalent of U.S. $400 but, because of the inflation, by the end of 18 months we would be paying close to $2,000 a month for it. I told the real estate agent about that house in Carapachay, owned by a man from the province of Gallego, in Spain. Her answer was, "Offer to pay the rent in U.S. dollars. The Gallegos love to have dollars." I offered U.S. $400 a month with an increase of 4 percent each month. The owner accepted the offer and we moved in.

We formed an evangelistic team composed of Jim and

Sharon Evans, and their teenage daughter, Brenda, and Ruth and I and our two teenage daughters, Karen and Cindy. Five Argentinians completed the team of 12: Carlos and Lissette DiLeo, Eduardo and Mary Colombo, and Clara Mirad.

The team started door-to-door visitation, and we held our first service in our living room on Easter Sunday 1979. Over the next 18 months, other Argentines plus ABWE missionaries Ronald and Christine Self were added to the team. During that time, with the help of Word of Life Institute students on the weekends, we rang more than 20,000 doorbells and presented the gospel to several hundred individuals. Scores made professions of faith in Christ, and many were baptized in a cement swimming pool in our backyard. In January 1981, the Missionary Baptist Church of Carapachay, in Buenos Aires, was organized with 25 charter members. God answered the prayers of those two women who prayed for ten years for a church to be started in their neighborhood.

When attendance was in the nineties, with other people receiving discipleship follow-up visits, we opened a branch work. We were on schedule in our projected growth. We had to move from our living room to the only place available, a banquet hall that usually cost $600 per night. The owner, influenced by the honesty of a Christian electrician, rented it to us for just $57 a night. Inflation quickly ran this up to $150, so we moved the church to an empty storefront showroom. We soon outgrew this place, but where could we go? We wanted to buy land and build, but we knew that would cost over $600,000. Before we left for Buenos Aires, God prompted us to pray for a building large enough to seat 1, 000. We needed a base strong enough to reach out to the city of Buenos Aires, the country of Argentina, and the world beyond. Jim Evans found a theater that had been up for sale for five years. It was centrally located, close to the railway station and five bus lines. But even considering buying this would be a step of faith. We had no money.

Our search for the theater's owner extended over many frustrating months. God allowed the delay so Pastor Dan Gelatt, of Elkhart, Indiana, and Pastor John White, of Calvary Baptist Church in Grand Rapids, Michigan, could visit us. When they saw the theater, they became excited about the possibility of buying it.

After more months of searching, a real estate agent who lived next door to the theater heard we were interested in the building. He found team member Carlos DiLeo and told him the asking price was $150,000. The realtor said he could put us in contact with the owner. But we had no money. Should we pursue the lead? Should we present this opportunity to ABWE administration for approval? God used Dan Gelatt, an ABWE board member, to help us. He presented the challenge to the ABWE board, and the purchase of the theater was approved. Then his church gave the first $5,000 toward the project.

We didn't know any of this until Bill Hopewell visited. He told Jim and me that the purchase of the theater was approved and the first $5,000 had been given. It seemed God was pushing us into this step of faith. I was assigned to deal with the real estate agent to negotiate the purchase.

During the first week of June 1980, the agent arranged a meeting with the theater owner at the property. I went with Eduardo Colombo and met the owner—a *woman*. No wonder we couldn't find the owner before. We had been searching for a man. We looked the building over and estimated it would be easy to put in 1,000 seats. Was this the auditorium we had prayed for? The agent asked us if we wanted to see the roof. We climbed a vertical ladder made of steel rungs fastened to the wall and went up through a hatch in the roof. Nothing was wrong with the roof. The real estate agent knew the owner wouldn't follow us, and he wanted to tell us the building's story.

Almost 11 years earlier, just after the two women began praying for a church in their suburb, the theater's original owner died. An inheritance battle among the man's children lasted for six years. One family member learned he was to get nothing from the sale of the building, so one night he spirited out all the seats and two projectors so it could no longer function as a theater. Shortly after the legal battle was settled, the area was re-zoned, placing the theater one-half block inside the residential area. Zoning laws allowed the building to be used as an auditorium, but without seats it wouldn't make a good theater. It couldn't be used as a dance hall because of the sloping floor. There it sat, empty. We were convinced God held it for His church. The agent asked us if we were interested in buying. We told him we needed to report to the church people and would get back to him. Really, we felt we needed more time to pray to make sure it was God's will we take this step of faith.

Days later on June 7, at 1:05 a.m., I suffered a severe heart attack. Ruth and I hadn't found a doctor yet, and didn't know where to contact an ambulance. Jim and Sharon Evans didn't have a phone, and other missionary colleagues lived far away. Ruth called the police station. They refused to help. She called the closest hospital, but there was no answer. Then I remembered the phone number of a taxi stand I had written down a few days before. Ruth called and was told no taxi was available for probably a half hour. Just as she was hanging up the phone, Ruth heard the man shout, "One has just arrived!" Ruth gave our address, and five minutes later the taxi was at the door.

Our daughter, Betty, had arrived to spend her summer vacation with us. By the time Ruth contacted the taxi, all three girls were awake and fluttering around in their nightgowns. When the taxi arrived, they called the driver to come in and help. He just stood looking at them. The two Bible institute students who were staying at our house that weekend carried me to the taxi. The driver took us to St. Vincent's Hospital, in Olivos, a neighboring suburb. The taxi was a little car with small wheels. It seemed the driver hit every bump along the way. I remembered that if severe pain during a heart attack lasts more than 20 minutes, the person would probably die. By this time, 30 minutes had passed.

In the taxi, I had an experience which was so precious to me I didn't tell anyone about it for a long time. A feeling of euphoria came over me, and I asked God, "Am I going home to be with You tonight?" I heard a voice saying clearly, "No, you are not coming home tonight, but you will have a new ministry." From there on I knew I wasn't going to die. I just wanted relief from the terrible pain in my chest and arms.

St. Vincent's Hospital had an intensive care unit where future cardiologists took their training. I was placed in this unit with IV medications dripping into my veins. The doctors would tell me, "You're doing fine." But then they would tell Ruth, "You have a very sick husband." The doctors expected I would suffer another heart attack. Although my pain diminished, it didn't cease until Sunday evening at 8:00 p.m., when it suddenly disappeared.

It was always difficult to make long distance calls out of Buenos Aires, especially on a Sunday. Betty spent five hours dialing her brother, David, in Brantford. She finally got through and told him of my heart attack. He called Pastor David Irwin at Central Baptist Church, in Brantford, and several other supporting churches. That evening many people prayed for me in their evening services, which finished around 8:00 p.m.—just when the pain stopped, and I was out of danger.

After nine days in intensive care, I was transferred to a general ward. A nurse wheeled me to the elevator. When the elevator door opened on the first floor, I saw a nurse and a doctor run into a room down the hallway. The nurse wheeled me to the doorway of that room, left me there, and walked into the room. It was drafty in the hallway. I was dressed only in the hospital gown and I was cold. A woman came out of the room and leaned against the doorjamb, crying. I thought, *How can I help this woman?* and prayed for direction. Then an idea came. I said to her, "I'm cold. Please help me put the pillows behind my back to protect me from the draft." She did this, then told me her husband had asthma and had stopped breathing. Just then a doctor came out of the room smiling. I told the woman her husband was all right. She asked, "How do you know?" I answered, "The doctor is smiling."

My nurse wheeled me into the room, which had three beds. I was in the middle one. On my left was the man with asthma. On the right was a man in multiple casts with a leg and one arm suspended in traction. He had been run over by a dump truck. A nurse laid out my nine medications on the bed stand and told me when to take them.

When the night nurse entered my room at 11:00 p.m., he told me he was the only nurse on the ward and had 50 patients to take care of. If I needed help, I was to yell because the call bell didn't work. I was too weak to yell. I couldn't remember when to take my medicine and was afraid I would take it at the wrong time. So I didn't take any. I had a fitful night with moans coming from the patient on my right, and wheezing from the asthmatic to my left.

The next day things got worse. People came and went all afternoon, visiting the asthmatic patient. I couldn't sleep. When Ruth appeared during visiting hours, I was crying and asked her to call Jim. "Get me out of here as soon as possible," I begged. The next morning, Jim arrived with an ambulance to take me to another hospital. The chief doctor at St. Vincent's wouldn't release me, as he hadn't seen me yet. He said, "Nor will I be able to for a couple of days." Jim spirited me out to the British Hospital.

My cardiologist was Dr. Humphreys, an Argentine of British descent. After looking over my medical reports, Dr. Humphrey asked me to tell him about one of my days. I began with rising at 6:00 a.m., and ended at 11:00 p.m. The whole day was filled with activities. He commented, "Your heart attack was obviously caused by stress." He kept me in the hospital for 10 days and told

Ruth I was not to hear anything about the work during my recuperation. He put me on a limited exercise program. I was taken completely out of the church-planting ministry.

That meant Jim and Eduardo had the responsibility of the negotiations for the theater building. This was God's design. I had experience in buying and selling property in Peru. Jim had none. He didn't know there were things you weren't supposed to do, he just did them.

Jim told me later about the theater purchase. The owner was asking U.S. $150,000, but hadn't received any purchase offers for five years. Members at our church told Jim to offer $80,000 and slowly increase the amount until the owner accepted. The real estate agent arranged a meeting at his office. Jim and Eduardo and the owner's husband—with his notary public—were there. In that meeting, Jim offered $80,000 for the building. The husband got angry, shouted he had never heard anything so stupid in his life, and stomped out of the office. All the others followed him to the sidewalk. They were out there arguing for five minutes before re-entering the office. The owner's husband told Jim, "All right, I'll sell for $90,000, but if it is in time payments, the price goes up to $100,000." Jim quietly told them, "I will take this offer back to the church members." Jim grasped that the owner was willing to sell on installments. We had never dreamed of this possibility, unheard of in Argentina, where interest rates ran at about 80 percent per year at that time.

The church members prayed and agreed that Jim should make an offer of time payments. Jim went back to the real estate agent and offered $20,000 down to get the keys, then $30,000 one month later, followed by two more payments of $25,000, the final one to be made in six months.

This time, the real estate agent stomped out to the sidewalk. He walked up and down, smoking, for five minutes. Then he calmed down and re-entered saying, "I have always wanted that building to be a church, and you are a church. But you also have to be the smartest businessmen in Buenos Aires. You have $50,000 in hand, and can invest it to make most of the money you need in interest." (Somehow he knew of the $5,000 we had received; and thought it was $50,000.) He told Jim, "I don't think the owner will accept, but I will take your offer to her." She accepted. Jim signed the contract and had one month to make the final decision to go ahead or not. The grand total: $100,000, plus another $10,000 for real estate fees and taxes. It was a lot of money!

I sat in our living room and prayed. Karen and Cindy restricted my visitors to five minutes each and made sure they said nothing about the church. This was hard for the visitors, especially the young men in training. But they obeyed. So I knew nothing about the negotiations.

Almost one month after Jim made his offer, he came to our house to receive a phone call from the ABWE office, which was to come through at 9:00 a.m. Jim didn't tell me what the call was about as he paced back and forth. By 10:45, his stomach was so upset he went home. He had forgotten about the two-hour time difference between Buenos Aires and Cherry Hill, New Jersey.

The phone rang at 11:00 a.m. I was the only one home, so I answered. ABWE's treasurer, Bill Pierson, and president, Wendell Kempton, were on the line. They asked for Jim, but since he wasn't there, they asked if I was up to answering questions about the theater. The men needed answers for a meeting that day. They asked 11 questions, mostly concerning who would own the building. Jim could not have answered many of the questions anyway, because I was the one working on ABWE's registration in Argentina.

The president and treasurer told me everything looked good for the approval of the purchase of the theater. Then Bill said, "A total of $20,000 has come in for the building, but you need to know that if all the money doesn't come in, you and Jim will be responsible for the balance." I calculated rapidly and figured we should be able to raise at least $60,000, so I asked Bill what the payments and interest would be on $50,000. He told me, said goodbye, and hung up. I stood there asking the Lord to provide all the money.

When the day for the first down payment arrived, Jim said, "I know you are not supposed to hear anything about the work, but I have to consult with you. I couldn't sleep last night. I spent the time in prayer and reading God's Word. The Spirit of God drew my attention to Psalm 118:5: *'I called upon the Lord in distress: the Lord answered me, and set me in a large place.'*"

The theater was a large place, and the money to buy it was a large amount. We spent the next two hours praying.

Clara Mirad was our church secretary. When the church approved the purchase with only $5,000 in hand, Clara thought it was the most stupid thing she had ever heard of. After our prayer time, Jim went out to the church office, which was in our backyard. Clara noticed that Jim was bothered about something. When Clara asked what was the matter, Jim said, "This is the hour of final decision. We are not sure we should proceed." Clara replied, "I think it would be a mistake to go back on it now. I read in the Psalms last night, and God gave me a verse." Clara then opened her Bible and read Psalm 118:5, the same verse Jim had read. When Jim told me this, I said, "That is the confirmation. Go and make the payment, and we will trust God for the rest."

At 1:00 p.m., Jim met with our lawyer, the owner and her lawyer, and our real estate agent. Jim said he would have the equivalent of $20,000 in Argentine funds in time for the 5:00 p.m. deadline. The owner spoke up, "No, I have always wanted the money in greenbacks (U.S. bills) and I won't receive it in any other way." The foreign exchange departments of the banks in Argentina close at 1:00 p.m. Where could Jim get $20,000 in U.S. bills after 1:00 p.m.?

Jim and the real estate agent went to a money-changer who told Jim to return at 4:00 p.m., as he had to count the bills he had taken in that day. Amazingly, he had received exactly U.S. $20,000. The money-changer accepted the ABWE check, and Jim presented the money to the owner. Jim said, "You should have seen the owner and her husband's faces. I think they thought we must have printed the money."

When the first $20,000 had been paid, the church launched into a faith program to purchase the theater. The unsaved realtor put up a large sign on the front of the vacant building, "SOLD, ACQUIRED BY THE MISSIONARY BAPTIST CHURCH."

But the battle for the building wasn't over. One month later, the second payment had to be made. The money-changer promised to have the necessary American cash on hand. At 1:00 p.m., on the afternoon of the payment, he told Jim, "I forgot to get the cash." The foreign exchange departments of the banks were closed. Things looked bleak, but God led Jim to a man in one of the banks who had the authority to release the money. The man was willing to help us because a pastor from our church had been used to rescue his son from drugs. He ordered the bank's foreign exchange department to cash our personal check and give us the American money, something done only for extremely important and well-known people. Our second payment was made on schedule.

Every week, I went to see my cardiologist. Dr. Humphreys was pleased with my progress but wanted me to get away for at least four months for a complete rest. He knew that if I stayed, I would be tempted to get back into the activities of the church. Rest areas in Argentina were too expensive for us, so we made plans to go to the United States and stay at the D & D Missionary Homes. Before those plans were finalized, I received a call from Pastor Dan Gelatt. He said, "I hear you have to take a few months rest. We have a home for you here in Elkhart. Your name is written over the door. Come and stay here."

On August 9, 1980, I was wheeled into the airport. I learned the fastest way to get through immigration and customs is to be taken through in a wheelchair. I was cleared right out to the waiting room where Ruth, Betty, Karen, and Cindy eventually met me.

We flew first to Lima. There we were told that the flight would not go on. We would have to continue on their flight to the United States the next day. This meant leaving the plane, going down a lot of steps, and staying overnight in Lima. The next day I slowly made my way back up all of those steps. Finally we arrived in Chicago, where ABWE missionaries Dave and Sandy Sizemore met us. They drove us in the church van to the house in Elkhart, arriving at 1:30 in the morning.

We immediately made a tour of the missionary house. It had new furniture and furnishings, wall-to-wall carpeting, piano, dishwasher, and an automatic washer and dryer. Karen remarked, "This must be what heaven is going to be like."

Dan Gelatt had arranged for an appointment with Dr. Plews, a cardiologist in Elkhart. He put me on a walking program and told me that if I didn't lose weight I would be in and out of the hospital for the rest of my life. That was all the motivation I needed for losing weight. I strictly followed the prescribed diet, and in six weeks lost 30 pounds, which I have kept off ever since.

On Saturday, August 23, 1980, the rest of our children arrived from Ontario. Tom and his wife, Kathy, brought their eight-month-old daughter, Jessica, so Ruth and I were able to meet our first grandchild.

Betty came from London, where she was attending London Baptist Seminary. Her roommate that year was Luda Gluchoman, a niece of Georgi and Nadia Vins. Georgi Vins was the much-respected Baptist pastor who had endured eight years in Soviet prisons because of his faith. Betty wanted us to go with her to meet the Vins family, who recently had settled in Elkhart. Twenty-two years later, Lisa (Vins) Carter shared her recollection of her first months in the United States. "In April 1979, my father was released from the Soviet Union as part of an exchange for spies. The government was happy to get rid of all of us, so my mother, grandmother, and the five children joined our father in America in July. By the time we met the Greenslades, the excitement of release from prison and coming to the United States had worn off. We didn't know how to relate to Americans. We were confused about the many different kinds of Christians. Pastor and Mrs. Greenslade visited us often. He was the first person we were really able to communicate with. He encouraged our family so much. In fact, my father said, 'It is amazing how much he understands us. It is as if we speak the same language.'"

We continued visiting the Vins family. A great friendship developed between Georgi and Nadia, and Ruth and me. We were able to help them through the initial culture shock of North America. Little did we know what adventures our meeting the Vins family would lead us into. It was through this friendship that ABWE opened a ministry among the unregistered churches in the Soviet Union.

Dan Gelatt found a used car with low mileage at an economical price. So we had four wheels with which to get around Elkhart and later to visit our churches. My cardiologist cleared me for limited travel. I wasn't allowed either by my doctor, or by ABWE, to raise money for the theater building. In fact, the ABWE office would not even tell me how much was still needed. They did not want me to feel any pressure. Dr. Plews told me, "Stop worrying about that money. God will send it in. Your job is to get better, so concentrate on that." In early November, I happened to read in a letter that of the $109,000 needed, $61,000 had been donated. Most of the funds came from people in churches that Jim and I did not even know.

In December, Dr. Plews sent me to St. Vincent's Hospital, in Indianapolis, for a complete checkup. By now I could walk three miles a day in 45 minutes. As a result of my walking program, I was able to stay on the treadmill for a full 15 minutes. Although tests showed a 95 percent blockage in one artery, the medical team decided that any man who could stay on the treadmill for 15 minutes does not need bypass surgery. They cleared me to return to Argentina because, as they said, "The man who taught us everything we know, Dr. Favaloro, is a doctor in Buenos Aires."

I was permitted to visit churches more extensively, so Ruth and I made a trip to Canada. At a missionary conference at West Park Baptist Church, in London, Ontario, a man handed me a check for $15,000—enough to make the final payment on the theater building in time for the closing date: January 12, 1981.

CHAPTER 18

Cardiac Care Church Planter

At the 1981 Missionary Enrichment Conference, Mel Cuthbert and I presented a paper on church planting and church growth. At the time, Mel and I both had heart problems, so we labeled ourselves "the cardiac care church planters."

My material was based on the premise that church-planting efforts often center on small, impoverished groups of people who are not able to start and maintain the work. As an alternative, I presented the study called "Strategy for Church Planting in Argentina." We began with a team made up of both North American and local Christian workers. Our goal was to build a large church—also called a mother church—that would be able to reproduce other churches. The process begins by starting many home Bible studies in strategic areas. These are held in various homes as an outreach ministry. As the home Bible studies grow, they are organized into feeder groups to enlarge the mother church. The mother church grows numerically and starts another church. This new church is made up of teams of commissioned workers from the mother church who work under the authority of the mother church until the new church is self-supporting.

I listed the advantages for using this plan:

• Local people are involved in leadership right from the start.

- The new church does not have to go through an identity crisis when it is thought to be "foreign." Instead, the new church has its own local identity from the beginning.
- The mother church can help the new work and provide resources that would not otherwise be available.
- The church starts with gifted and trained people who know how to run a church.
- A spirit of cooperation is developed among churches.
- Well-trained men and women have a wider scope in which to use their abilities.

In later years, some of the material Mel and I presented was included in the ABWE publication *Church Planter's Manual,* a book of practical ideas for starting churches. This book continues to be used as a guide for church planters.

Ruth and I left Brantford for Miami, and flew to Buenos Aires on August 30, 1981. Karen and Cindy were with us. Betty was studying at London Baptist Seminary. Dave was teaching school in Baltimore, Maryland, and Kathy in Parma Heights, Ohio, near Cleveland. In November 1981 Tom, was called to pastor Cannington Baptist Church, northeast of Toronto.

Before our departure, Wendell Kempton told me we could return to Argentina, as long as I restricted myself to half of my normal workload. My cardiologist had ordered me out of active church planting. That meant no door-to-door visitation, no discipleship, no counseling, and no direct administration. He said, "There is too much stress in all of these. It is time for you to sit back in the general's chair and send younger men into the trenches."

This was a time of much prayer and heart searching. We had committed ourselves to Argentina for at least 10 years, but the question was, Should we stay there if my church-planting work was limited? If we did not stay, what should we do? Slowly we realized what my new ministry would be.

Bill Hopewell asked me to serve as a counselor for the field councils in Chile and Paraguay. I made frequent trips to those countries to work with the missionaries. Part of the planning was to arrange for continuity of the work. This included assuring adequate missionary coverage at any given time. I also became counselor to the young church planters in Argentina. I visited them every week, guiding them in church planting. I listened to the missionaries and church planters, recommended procedures, encouraged them, and prayed for them. This ministry was fulfilling and within the limits of my diminished physical capacities.

During the early months of 1982, world attention focused on Argentina because of the Falkland Islands. This string of sparsely inhabited islands passed among French, Spanish, and British rule. In 1892, British colonial status was granted to the Falklands. Argentina calls the islands *Las Islas Malvinas* and regularly protests British occupation. On April 2, 1982, Argentina's military government invaded the Falklands. The war ended 10 weeks later with the surrender of the Argentine forces to British troops, who had forcibly reoccupied the islands. Argentina still claims the islands, but an agreement between Argentina and the United Kingdom in 1995 sought to defuse sovereignty conflicts that would dampen foreign interest in the Falkland's potential oil reserves.

I was in the British Hospital for a few days during the Falkland War. Several police were stationed to protect the hospital. They covered the name, "British Hospital" with a large Argentine flag. The entire board and staff of the hospital were Argentinian.

In the summer of 1984, we spent a brief furlough in Ontario, headquartering in London, and living for a while in a dorm at the London Baptist Bible College. Karen and Cindy entered Bible college in September. Kathy left to begin her service as an ABWE missionary to Peru. We returned to Buenos Aires on September 11, 1984.

Now Ruth and I had to adjust to being without any of our children after having them with us for 30 years. Karen and Cindy's friend, Miriam Miguens, had boarded with us on weekends while attending Word of Life Bible Institute. She now moved in with us, became our adopted daughter, and helped fill the gap left by our children's absence.

During that short time in Canada, I qualified for my ham radio license and applied for one in Argentina. Having that license made it possible for us to communicate with our children. We are grateful for the various "Hams" who helped us keep in contact with family members.

In February 1985, we traveled to Santiago, Chile, for an All ABWE Southern Cone Conference with 108 ABWE missionaries, national pastors, wives, and families. They came from Paraguay, Uruguay, Argentina, and Chile. Each morning was spent in classes, round-table discussions, and prayer, and each afternoon was free for siesta, sports, handcrafts, and other events. Rev. Hamilton, missionary from Ireland, gave challenging messages each evening on the importance of prayer. He left for Santiago Saturday night, and I was to bring the closing message on Sunday night. However, God brought the message instead of me.

During the conference in Santiago, all of us felt several tremors. In the two weeks prior to our arrival, over 200 tremors shook the ground. In one evening message, Rev. Hamilton said, "What we need is a touch from God." At that moment, the whole building shook. It was impressive. The next day we were all in the dining hall enjoying our evening meal when the earth began to tremble. The man in charge of the campgrounds told us to stay seated, be calm, and wait for the quake to pass. Only it didn't pass quickly, as he said it would. Instead, tables moved, windows shook, walls swayed in and out, and the roof rose up and down. All of the kitchen equipment—pots and pans, and dishes—were thrown to the floor. Walls cracked, and a big hole appeared in the roof. It was time to get out of the dining hall.

The first one out the door was the man in charge of the camp. In the rush, people pushed and shoved in front of us, pushing chairs aside. I tripped over one and fell flat on my face. The ground around me began to open and close right under my nose, so I got out of there in a hurry. We all found an open space where we could keep away from electric lines and other dangers. The quake lasted four minutes and measured 7.8 on the Richter scale. When it stopped, we put chairs from the dining hall in the open space and prayed for churches holding services at that time. Then the second earthquake came, 10 minutes after the first. This measured 8.2 on the Richter scale. Walls began to crumble and buildings toppled over. The wheels of a van rose right off the ground.

Local people knew we could not stay in the cabins because of aftershocks. We pulled out mattresses and took them to the open space. We made a bonfire and endeavored to sleep under the stars. We didn't get much sleep, however, because every few minutes repeat quakes, some of them measuring as high as 6, made our mattresses flop up and down and woke us up. There was also the danger of a tidal wave, but that did not happen, for which we thank God.

The earthquake left 60 percent of the houses in a nearby town damaged and uninhabitable. Over 2,000 people were injured; 200,000 were left homeless, and 200 were killed. I was the only person injured among our 108, when I scraped my shins on the chair I fell over.

In spite of assisting in various countries, our hearts were still in the work of establishing churches in Argentina's capital area. In May 1985, our team added another church plant on the south side of Buenos Aires in a section called Bernal. God allowed Ruth and me to take part in the formation of this church. Ismael Cajal and his wife, Alicia, both graduates of the Word of Life Bible Institute, were the moving force behind this new group. Ruth and I began working with them each weekend to help bring the group to the status of an organized church.

Each Saturday morning, Ruth and I rode by train into the center of the city, transferred to a subway, and then to another train. The trip generally took at least two hours. Cars were expensive to buy and maintain in Argentina, so we always traveled by public transportation. That was the tiring part of my ministry.

We stayed overnight in Bernal with a local family, and ministered in the church on Saturday evening and Sunday. My main responsibility was guiding Ismael and the church leaders. I taught them about the responsibilities of deacons and church members, practices and procedures in the church, and Baptist distinctives.

The Bernal church plant grew by 150 percent in one year and organized into the Missionary Baptist Church of Bernal. We rejoiced as Ismael and others grew in stature and capabilities in their church work. I continued to teach each weekend on how a church functions, and helped the pastor and the two deacons in any way they wanted me to help.

In March, we received news that Karen had received a diamond ring in February and was planning to be married October 12, 1985, to Grant Verdoold, a fourth-year student at London Baptist Bible College. Both Karen and Cindy graduated from the two-year program at the Bible college. With the help of Christian friends, Ruth and I made a fast trip to Canada for the wedding.

After returning to our base in Argentina, I continued my travels to Chile, Paraguay, and Peru. Both Ruth and I went to Peru in January 1986, where I spoke at a conference of ABWE missionaries and pastors in Arequipa. We also went to Nazca to take part in Magdalena Barrera's wedding. Magdalena had lived with us for three years in Iquitos while attending Iquitos Baptist Bible Institute. Our daughter Kathy participated in the wedding. She was teaching ABWE missionary children in Ica, a four-hour drive south of Lima. She and Magdalena worked together in the seminary in Ica. After the wedding, Ruth spoke at a ladies' camp in Pisco on the Pacific coast near Ica. We flew to Iquitos for further ministries, returning to Buenos Aires on February 7, 1986.

Everything was going well for me. I did not feel unusual pressure or stress related to the church ministries. Then in 1986, I began having angina pains. I couldn't walk more than four blocks without having to sit down and rest.

I underwent a battery of tests at the British Hospital, which used ultra-modern equipment purchased from the United States. The angiogram showed four blockages in my arteries, one 95 percent blocked. Dr. Humphreys said, "You urgently need bypass surgery because you could die at any moment."

I had confidence in the abilities of the Argentine surgeons. Dr. Favaloro, a heart surgeon in Buenos Aires is one of the pioneers in developing bypass surgery. The cardiac staff is highly trained and capable. Yet, as I talked matters over carefully with Dr. Humphreys, I said, "This is a serious operation. Perhaps I should go to Canada to be close to my family and supporting churches." He agreed, and Ruth and I began to plan for our return to Canada.

This meant terminating our church-planting work in Argentina. Within three days, we were ready to leave. I gave Jim Evans power of attorney to sell our house. Church youth helped us pack. I sat in the living room and watched. We made three piles: one to keep and ship, one to sell, another to give away. As the young people brought the things in, I pointed to one of the piles. The give-away pile was soon gone. Jim offered to pack into barrels the things to be shipped to Canada.

We left Buenos Aires on October 16, 1986, amidst a lot of farewell tears, because everyone knew this was the end of our full-time ministry in Argentina. We flew all night with stops in Chile and Peru, and arrived in Toronto the following morning. Our children who were living in Ontario met us at the airport and took us to Brantford.

Dr. Young, our family doctor, arranged an appointment for me with a heart specialist. I took along all the information and test reports from Buenos Aires. The doctor looked them over and wanted to consult with others. I returned one week later to hear the results. The medical team asked a lot of questions, then decided they could not do the bypass surgery because of the location of the blockages. They prescribed further medication and told me to return in six months. This was a big disappointment, because I felt that with surgery I would regain my strength and be able to continue in the ministry.

I endeavored to help Rev. Reg Snell, the ABWE Canadian representative, in office work and representing the mission in churches. My weakness, however, increased until I was unable to work more than two or three hours a day. I asked Dr. Young if there wasn't something that could be done. He sent me to Dr. Bate, an internist in Brantford, who said the same thing I was told in Buenos Aires. "In looking over the angiogram film and reading the reports on your tests, I see you urgently need help. You could die at any minute." He made an appointment with leading cardiologists, and on March 29, 1987, I was admitted to the Toronto General Hospital. They looked over the film from Buenos Aires, did another angiogram, and decided on angioplasty, the balloon expansion of the blockage in the arteries. On April 1, they did that procedure on four arteries. This was the first time it had been done on more than two arteries at one time. This procedure gave me a new lease on life. The first day I was allowed up, I felt as if I had springs in my legs. The doctors told me I would soon be able to continue a full ministry. That was wonderful news, but raised the question: "Where?"

Ruth and I realized we could no longer be directly involved in the rigors of church planting, but we could help other church planters in various countries. We could also represent ABWE in churches in North America. That is how we began in the summer of 1987. We traveled extensively visiting churches in the northern United States and in Canada.

At the mission's annual Missionary Enrichment Conference in July, we had the joy of seeing our daughter Kathy accepted by

ABWE as a full-time MK teacher, assigned to Colombia. We rejoiced in developments in two of our other daughters' lives as well. In May 1987, Cindy graduated from London Baptist Seminary and on August 22, 1987, married David Middleton. That same year, Karen gave birth to her first son, Jeremy.

In addition to my medical problems, we believe the Lord took us back to Ontario at this time to help care for Ruth's parents. We lived in their house between trips to Bible colleges and churches. Ruth cooked, cleaned, and shopped. I helped keep their medications straight. Later, Ruth was able to help move her parents into a nursing home.

At my final cardiac checkup in Toronto, in September, I was cleared for international travel. We saw the answer to the "Where?" question. We headquartered in Ontario and planned to travel to *wherever* we were needed.

CHAPTER 19

"And Beyond"

In 1986, Rev. David and Rosezell Stevenson visited Europe, where they were especially moved by the lack of Christian workers in Italy. The Stevensons applied to ABWE and were accepted in the 1987 candidate class, pending the ABWE board's decision to open Italy as a field of service. On January 28, 1988, I traveled with Jesse Eaton, ABWE administrator for Europe, board member Larry Fetzer, and David Stevenson to survey that country.

We met with missionaries from various mission agencies in order to get a picture of the spiritual needs of Italy and determine what areas most needed missionaries. We learned that 99 percent of the population is Roman Catholic, although only a small percentage practice their religion. Of 32,000 towns and cities, only 1,000 had any kind of evangelical witness. We gathered a large amount of information, and the ABWE board voted to open Italy to ABWE missionaries.

On returning to Brantford, Ruth and I signed for the purchase of a home. This was possible because of a little equity from our house in Argentina and the help of a Christian couple we knew from childhood. They gave us a $1,000 personal gift because they had not been able to support us throughout our years in South America. We never expected to own a house. We thought we would either live in low rental housing or in a house trailer. We learned again that we can never outgive God.

In 1988, the ABWE Canadian Council considered opening

Canada as a mission field and asked me to conduct the country survey. Ruth and I began with a trip to the western provinces of Canada.

Our Canadian fact-finding mission was interrupted when the missionaries in Ica, Peru, phoned, requesting I help them in some important decisions and in setting goals for the coming year.

We then resumed our Canadian survey trip by visiting New Brunswick and Nova Scotia from mid-October to mid-November. While in New Brunswick, we received a call from our daughter Karen, who told us that her 18-month-old son, Jeremy, had been taken by ambulance to the Sick Children's Hospital in Toronto, where he was diagnosed with leukemia. Ruth flew immediately to be with Karen. After a few days in the cancer ward, the medical staff decided it wasn't leukemia and moved Jeremy to another floor. This was a great relief to Karen, but from all the stress she went into early labor, and Rebecca was born a month early. Jeremy was still hospitalized in Toronto, while Karen was in the hospital in Richmond Hill, an hour away. All survived, and I joined Ruth as soon as possible. Jeremy's problem was never diagnosed, but we thank God he recovered.

Our findings about Canada revealed that the country is the largest in the Western Hemisphere and second largest in the world. Twenty-five cities have populations of 100,000 or more, and Toronto, Montreal, and Vancouver are mega-cities. We also discovered that while many people would consider themselves Christians, secularization and pluralization affect all levels of society. The ABWE board, in conjunction with the Canadian Council, voted to inaugurate an active evangelism and church-planting ministry in Canada.

In December 1988, I joined Jesse Eaton, Ralph Gruenburg, executive director of projects, and ABWE board member Mark Jackson, to determine the spiritual needs of Germany. We spent two weeks in consultation with missionaries from various agencies and with German believers. After hearing our report, the

ABWE board voted to enter the country of Germany to establish churches.

I lined up at the check-in counter at the airport for my flight back to Canada. Next to our counter was another line of people checking in on Pan Am flight 103. When news that the Pan Am aircraft blew up over Lockerbie, Scotland, many people from Central Baptist Church worried, wondering if that was my flight. By the grace of God, it wasn't. I returned to Ontario safely.

On May 16, 1989, Ruth and I joined a team flying to the Soviet Union to make contact with the unregistered Baptist churches. In the early 1960s, the atheistic Soviet government forced on Christians a set of regulations that contradicted Scripture. Fearing reprisals, the majority of church leaders complied with the government. In 1961, a group of Baptist preachers took a stand to defend biblical truth, and independent churches were established all over the Soviet Union. They refused to register with the Soviet government and functioned as underground churches, holding services and camps hidden from the authorities. They also formed an Association of Unregistered Churches, of which Georgi Vins was secretary. He was arrested and served eight years in Siberian prison camps along with many other pastors of unregistered churches.

This trip to the Soviet Union came about through our friendship with Georgi Vins, who played a major role in setting up our schedule. Our fellow team members were Wendell and Ruth Kempton; Mary Smallenberger (now Wooten), who was our interpreter; and Dona Jaeger, from Chicago. My wife insisted on going because if they put me in prison, she wanted to be with me. I told her she would be in a different prison, but she still wanted to go along.

Our tourist agent, George Johnson, met us in Helsinki, Finland. He had rented a big white van. Ours was the only white van we saw on the roads in Russia. People stopped to look at us everywhere we went. The Russian Intourist Company laid out our itinerary, including the cities we could visit and the hotels where we could stay. We knew our rooms were bugged because when we said something was broken in the room, within a few minutes, a repairman arrived to fix it. We were allowed to stay in two cities for two nights. In all of the others, we could stay only one night. Regulations limited us to a maximum of 311 miles (500 km) travel each day.

Ruth wrote:

> We were a little nervous crossing the border, not knowing what might happen. The Lord wonderfully answered prayer. They took our Christian literature, New Testaments, and Bibles into another room and then brought them all out, saying, "These people are evangelicals, they aren't going to do us any harm," and gave the books back. Just a month before, officials had confiscated all the literature from another group. When we crossed on the way back, they didn't even open our suitcases, just searched the van from top to bottom, putting it over a pit to examine it from underneath.

> We traveled 3,500 miles (5,633 kms) visiting cities where there were unregistered churches. When we reached each city, we looked for the hotel, registered, and then set out to find our contact person. Some of these cities had a population of three to six million and no city map. The Lord led us step by step, and we were able to find the right apartment building and the right rooms. Some of the buildings had 400 or more apartments and were not numbered according to the floors. We had to guess which floor to go to. We knocked at the door; Mary gave the Russian Christian greeting and asked if we could talk to them. They immediately let us in without knowing who we were. After explaining who we were and why we were there, they insisted on feeding us. They cried and talked and talked. We seldom arrived back at our hotel room before 1:30 a.m. Many mornings we had to leave early in order to reach the next city by suppertime. There were no gas stations, restaurants, lunch stops, or rest rooms along the highways; but

there were trees on both sides, so the men went to one side of the highway and the ladies to the other. We held meetings in Leningrad, Moscow, Orel, Kharkov, Kiev, and Minsk.

These were the two busiest weeks of our missionary career. God protected us and gave us the health and strength we needed. He also gave us the privilege of meeting Christians who spent many years in prison for preaching. Many, with tears in their eyes, said we were the first people from North America to visit them.

Our reason for going to the Soviet Union was to encourage believers to reach out to their own people in church planting and evangelism. Pastors said, "We have just been surviving. We don't know how to evangelize in a more open society. Teach us." Many years ago Bibles and Christian literature were confiscated. Some pastors didn't even have a Bible. Now with Bibles and literature coming into the country, they said, "You have given us back our hands." The pastors thanked all those who wrote letters or sent Bibles and literature to them while in prison. Their request still is, "Please send more." Unsaved people are asking for Bibles and New Testaments; thousands are needed.

We returned to Canada, where I was named Canadian representative for ABWE. At that time, ABWE was enlarging its efforts to reach into the Eastern European countries. Dr. Kempton asked me to act as "point man" in North America, coordinating trips for ministry and teaching in those countries. Ruth and I were studying Russian from a course on cassette tapes in preparation for more trips to the Soviet Union.

We left in the middle of April 1990 for our second trip into Russia. The others in our group were: Michael Loftis, then an ABWE missionary in Germany; Marc Blackwell, ABWE missionary in South Africa; Mary Smallenberger; Diane Somerville, from Brantford; and John Poulson, pastor of Wealthy Park Baptist Church, in Grand Rapids, Michigan. We each carried three heavy suitcases containing Russian literature and New Testaments. We had difficulty at customs but, finally, around 3:00 a.m., after negotiating for three hours, we were allowed to take everything with us. We drove over 3,728 miles (6,000 kms), pulling a trailer containing the suitcases.

In each city, we had to stay in the Intourist Hotel, where the rooms were bugged. We had to be very careful of what we said. In one church, we were the first North Americans ever to visit. Each church service lasted three hours, with four preachers. There were no backs on the benches, yet the churches were filled to capacity, with many standing. We took part in two rallies in the "forest," as the wooded parks on the outskirts of the city were called. Around 1,000 people attended the first service and 2,500 were at the second, which lasted seven hours, with band music, choirs, orchestras, solos, poetry, and several preachers. In both rallies, most of the people stood the entire time. When the invitation was given, 62 people came forward for salvation.

During the two weeks, 119 unsaved people responded to the invitation to receive Christ. If the choir or congregation was singing, or the band playing, or someone was preaching, they stopped in mid-verse or mid-sentence and dealt with those who came forward. They all knelt at the front. A microphone was placed before them. Their voices were sent out over the entire area on powerful public address systems. Most of them wept with tears of repentance and remorse for sins, praying sometimes for as long as five minutes. When they finished, one of the pastors or church leaders prayed for them, then the service resumed.

We were able to meet with pastors, children's workers, and young peoples' leaders for teaching, answering their many questions, and encouraging them. Bible-believing Christians in Russia told us they were taking advantage of the "illegal freedom" they had. The old repressive laws were still on the books, but authorities did not apply them. Thus, believers were able to hold church services, open-air rallies in parks, and distribute literature on the streets.

One unique method of evangelism was a "loaning library," set up in places where people strolled on Saturdays or Sundays. Large banners were displayed. Bibles, New Testaments, Gospels of John, and other books were loaned for two weeks to those who registered with their government I.D. card and address. These people were invited to a special service held the same evening to answer their questions and present the gospel. Many were saved each week through this method.

On leaving the Soviet Union, Ruth and I visited France. I accompanied three ABWE missionaries, John Weeks, Tim Weeks, and Dennis Toll on a 12-day trip by van to locate church-planting opportunities and to learn more about the country. Ruth stayed in Caen with Amy Toll, helping her take care of her three small children. One of them asked Ruth, "Will you be my grandma while you are here?"

After three weeks in France, we took the train to Madrid, Spain, counseling with missionaries and helping where we could. France and Spain are hard countries to evangelize because it takes many years to gain the confidence of the people. Missionaries used youth centers and sports programs as a way to reach people.

On July 1, 1990, our daughter Karen gave birth to Benjamin, a month early. He had no lining in the air sacs of his lungs. He was flown immediately by helicopter to Sick Children's Hospital, in Toronto, where he was attached to many tubes including one in each big toe. He underwent an experimental treatment in which the lining from a cow's lung was injected into his lungs. Three months later, Betty gave birth to Thomas, who had the same problem and underwent the same treatment. It worked! Benjamin and Thomas are now healthy 12-year-olds.

The following February, we joined Mel and Romilda Cuthbert as part of a team going to Romania for evangelism, meeting government officials, and planning ABWE's ministry in that country. Romanian church leaders asked for missionaries who had experience to guide and work with them, training church planters and pastors, and forming churches in order to care for the large number of new believers.

We stayed with a Christian family, Mihai and Chivuta Vaidos and their three children, on the tenth floor of an apartment building. Mihai was a foreman at a large factory. His wage was U.S. $38.00 a month. We found the homes were nicely furnished and had lovely china and crystal, all of which had been purchased many years before. People now had a hard time economically because of high inflation with no increase in wages.

We visited several towns and villages, speaking through interpreters in four churches. In Targu Mures, a city of 200,000, the Second Baptist Church met in a second-floor room loaned to them by the local Red Cross. The room held about 100 people, any more and the floor would have given way. We found it easy to distribute tracts in Romania. People ran to get them.

Early in 1993, Dr. Michael Loftis, now president of ABWE, contacted us about working with the unregistered Baptist churches in Ukraine for two months. He told us, "People in the former Soviet Union greatly respect and listen to older people. We need a gray-haired missionary on site to encourage a key Baptist church to accept the ministries ABWE offers. If the members receive you, they will receive our mission." I asked Dr. Loftis what we should do. He answered, "Just be there."

We flew into Budapest, Hungary, on January 30. After a couple of days there to get accustomed to the time change, Michael Loftis drove us to Kiev, Ukraine, a two-day journey by van. The weather was so cold that fog froze on the trees.

Kiev is a city of over two million. We were unable to find an apartment at first, so arrangements were made for us to stay with an unsaved couple. He was a trainer in Olympic rifle and pistol competitions. Both he and his wife had many medals. Some of his students won silver medals and the teams won gold medals in the Olympics.

Later, we rented a small, furnished apartment in Kiev for

U.S. $90.00 a month, including heat and utilities. It was on the fifth floor, and many times the small, rickety elevator did not work. The hallways and stairways were usually dark—people stole the light bulbs. We had to have a flashlight with us if we were returning at night. We washed our clothes by hand in the bathtub and hung them in the bathroom. The apartment was heated with pipes, and the temperature could not be adjusted. We were glad we had taken a roll of masking tape with us. We taped around the windows to keep the cold out. The temperature was −4°F (−20°C) for two weeks.

A few days after our arrival, we met with one of the pastors of the church, who was to find out all he could about us for presentation to the church. When he found we were fluent in Spanish, he said, "This is the main reason why our church should work with ABWE." He told us of Dr. Jorge, an unsaved Spanish-speaking doctor who was attending their church. Ruth and I were excited about the opportunity to share the gospel in Spanish again.

We did not have a Spanish Bible with us since it had not crossed our minds we might need one. We faxed the ABWE–Canada office, requesting they send my Spanish Bible. I wanted the one I used for preaching, and explained where it was located in our house. The office could send it with an ABWE missionary coming to teach in a seminar. The Bible reached the missionary one hour before his departure, and two days later he handed it to me at a pastoral training seminar. It wasn't the Bible I requested, but a newer one. This was disappointing because I was more familiar with my old one. However, it was what I needed: a Spanish Bible.

Ruth and I met Dr. Jorge the following Sunday. What a delight for all of us to be talking in Spanish in Ukraine! Right away, we felt as if we were old friends. We didn't know it at the time, but we were in for one of the greatest experiences of our missionary career.

We arranged to visit Dr. Jorge the next afternoon to learn about his background. Educated in Jesuit elementary and high schools, as a university student Dr. Jorge lost faith in the official church of his country because he saw it did not help or take care of the needs of poor people, even though the church was affluent. He became active in a communist organization and was soon one of the leaders. Every year, the Soviet Communist Party offered scholarships to the top ten students. He qualified, and went to the Soviet Union with great expectations. He said, "I thought myself on the way to paradise. That is what we were always taught." He told of his great disappointment in what he found—the immorality in all walks of life and the corruption and backwardness the communist system created.

He made trips with other Latin American students into Western Europe. They played their guitars and sang. People listened and tossed coins into their open guitar cases. He saw the superiority of the economy and freedom in the Western countries. All this led to his disenchantment with the communist system.

He was sent to the Soviet Union to become a dental technician, but his marks were so high they transferred him to medicine. While studying, he married a Russian nurse. He graduated from medical school but, as a general practitioner, wasn't allowed to stay in the Soviet Union. He returned to Peru to practice medicine for one year. He feared terrorists would find out he no longer believed in communism and kill him. Letters from his wife told how their daughters were being affected by the immorality in the schools. Caught between these problems, he returned to the Soviet Union and specialized in urology. As a specialist, he was able to remain in the country.

Dr. Jorge told us of his search for truth and also stated he had returned to Roman Catholicism. About two years before we met him, he and his wife decided they needed a good church in which to raise their three daughters. They felt this was the only way they could avoid having their daughters taken in by the immorality in their school and in the whole country. They attended various churches, but did not find what they were looking for.

When Dr. Jorge's wife changed jobs, she asked one of her new co-workers, "Do you know of a good church where we can raise our daughters?" This woman was from the unregistered Baptist church, and invited Dr. Jorge's wife to go with her to church. She went, taking her three daughters with her. After she was saved, she requested baptism.

Pastors visited Dr. Jorge to ask his permission to baptize his wife. The doctor agreed, and attended his wife's baptism. He was impressed with the singing and the upright young people. He, too, began attending church. The pastors talked with him of spiritual things, trying to lead him to trust Christ, but without success. Dr. Jorge thought he was right with God because of his good works.

Among the regulations Christians were required to sign was one stating that atheism and evolution were true. When they refused to sign, they were not allowed to receive medical treatment, which was controlled by the state. Believers did the best they could, using home remedies, but church members prayed for years that God would send them a Christian doctor to set up a clinic in the church. Now there was a doctor in their midst, but he was unsaved. Then the members prayed that God would send a Spanish-speaking believer who could lead Dr. Jorge to the Lord. By faith they trusted God for the doctor's conversion and for their medical clinic.

When Dr. Jorge told me he had returned to his old beliefs, I asked, "Then you believe in God?" He answered, "Yes." I asked, "But He is far away, isn't He?" Again he answered, "Yes." I suggested we meet in his home every Monday and Friday afternoon so I could show him how he could get close to God. Dr. Jorge was pleased with the idea. On our first visit, I loaned him my Spanish Bible and instructed him to start reading the gospel of

John. During the next four days, he read John, Acts, and into the book of Romans. I realized bringing the "wrong" Bible was all part of God's plan. I was able to give the new Bible to Dr. Jorge as a gift.

Dr. Jorge's annual vacation fell during the month of March. For the first time in years, the family decided to stay at home instead of going on a trip because his wife would soon give birth. This allowed more time for Dr. Jorge to study the Bible, to show us around the city, to help us with our shopping, and to interpret for us. When Ruth developed a sore throat, he became our personal family doctor.

In our Bible studies, he interpreted what we said in Spanish into Russian for the benefit of his family. He invited a doctor friend to his house one evening and interpreted as I presented the gospel to his friend. At the same time, he was hearing the gospel message and telling it to someone else. He chuckled and said, "I'm preaching, and I'm not even saved. I think God wants me to be a preacher."

March 15, 1993, was crucial in the lives of this family. I decided they had received sufficient teaching on the way of salvation, so instead of a Bible study, I asked them if they had any questions. The doctor's 16-year-old daughter voiced her objection to the biblical teaching of wives being subject to their husbands. She asked, "What if he is lazy? What if he is a drunken man? What if he is an abusive husband?" We discussed this topic for some time. She was unsaved and had an unsaved boyfriend. Her parents were trying to get her to break up with him. She told us he was the nicest boy in the world, and she didn't want to terminate the relationship.

After 30 minutes, I saw I couldn't answer her questions to her satisfaction. So I asked her if she would go to heaven if she died that night. She answered, "No." I asked her if she would like to go. She answered, "Yes." I began a process of showing her how she could be assured of going to heaven. She was already familiar with most of what I was talking about because of the teaching and preaching she heard in church. I sensed she was reluctant to make a decision because she knew she would have to break up with her unsaved boyfriend, who was not interested in attending church.

We came to the final questions. "Do you understand what I'm talking about?" She answered, "Yes." I asked if she wanted to make a decision at that moment. She and her father looked at each other. The doctor previously told me he would make a decision for Christ when his daughter did. I sensed they were both considering this. Then the doorbell rang! They all headed out into the foyer to the front door. I thought, *Oh, Lord, why this interruption?* We were soon to find out.

Her boyfriend was there with his mother and accused the doctor's daughter of stealing money from a fund the students were collecting. She hadn't done this, and was able to prove it to them. God used this incident to show her that her boyfriend wasn't so wonderful after all.

Meanwhile, Ruth and I were praying. I said to Ruth, "When they come back in, I'm going to zero in on Jorge." She answered, "I think you should." They came back into the room. I turned to the doctor and asked him if he was ready to receive Christ. He answered, "I knew you were going to ask that." He and his daughter chatted back and forth in Russian. He told me that her boyfriend was no longer an issue, as she saw what he was really like. She wanted to receive Christ. He said he did, too. We all knelt. She asked Christ into her life. He interpreted her prayer into Spanish so we would understand. Then he prayed in Spanish, confessing his sins and accepting Christ, interpreting his prayer into Russian for his family. We got up from our knees rejoicing.

Then his wife said their youngest, an eight-year-old girl had wanted to do this for a long time. So they called her in. We all knelt again, and she accepted Christ. We got up and chatted for

a while about what had happened. Then the oldest girl told us
her 13-year-old sister was out in the kitchen crying because she
wanted to accept Christ, too. They called her in. Again we knelt
as she received Christ. What a time of rejoicing! The family was
now united in Christ.

The following Sunday, the four of them stood in front of
the church to tell the congregation what had happened. They
requested baptism. Three other people went forward for baptism,
and four others went forward for salvation. There was hardly a
dry eye in the whole church.

Dr. Jorge's mother-in-law attended the next Bible study in
his house. She had made a profession of faith a few months before, but now told us a sad tale of hearing voices all her waking
hours—voices telling her what to do and where to go. She suffered from bad dreams at night. We recognized this demonic
influence, prevalent in the former Soviet Union. We had dealt
with similar situations many times in Peru. After hearing her
story, I asked her if she would go to heaven if she died tonight.
She replied, "No." I said, "Then that is your real problem. Let's
take care of that first." Step by step Ruth and I led her to true
faith in Christ.

I told her she was listening to demons, which was sin. I told
her when she knelt to receive Christ she must confess this and
renounce all relationship with the voices. She did this in a simple, heartfelt prayer, confessing her sin and receiving eternal life
in Christ. At the supper table, she told us the voices were gone.
We saw her several times in the following weeks. She was a smiling Christian with victory in her life—and no more problems
with voices.

Today, Dr. Jorge is a preacher and a deacon in the church. He
and his wife are active in their church. He also has an effective
evangelistic ministry, especially among medical people. He con-
ducts medical clinics in various churches; his wife and oldest
daughter, both nurses, work with him. These medical clinics are

part of an evangelism, church planting, and discipleship outreach.

There are no accidents with God. Ruth and I were in the place God wanted us to be at the right time. Obeying Him always pays off.

At the end of 1993, Rev. Frank Bale, who, with his wife, Brenda, served as an ABWE missionary in Brazil and Portugal, became the director of ABWE–Canada. I retained the title of "Representative." Ruth and I continued traveling to different ABWE fields, encouraging and guiding missionaries and pastors in evangelism, church planting, and training leaders. In 1994, we spent two months in Turin, Italy, a month in Romania, six weeks in Argentina, and two months in Ukraine.

We returned to Buenos Aires for three months in 1995 to help Missionary Baptist Church, in Bernal, celebrate its tenth anniversary. I was privileged to speak at Ismael Cajal's ordination. In September, we returned once again to Argentina, and stayed until December of that year. Ruth's sister and her husband, Mary Anne and Floyd Pirie, joined us. During their three-week stay, they provided music and led the children's program at the Southern Cone Missionary Conference, in Asuncion, Paraguay, for missionaries from Chile, Argentina, and Paraguay. While visiting the churches in Argentina, Floyd and Mary Anne sang several times and she played her violin. People at Bernal especially enjoyed her playing. Some told us they had heard violin music on the radio and TV but had never seen anyone play one.

In 1996, I went to Ukraine for 12 days to teach at the Odessa Training Center, where Canadian ABWE missionary John Taylor serves. Of the 35 pastors and leaders who attended the classes, one was Dr. Jorge.

We planned to return to Ukraine, but I had more heart problems and had to have another angiogram. I spent most of the month of April in and out of Toronto General Hospital. On May 6, I had angioplasty along with the insertion of a stent to ensure the artery would stay open. The doctors told me I was suffering from congestive heart failure and needed to slow down and make changes in my lifestyle.

In 1997, we returned to Argentina for six weeks. Three of these were in the city of Lobos, where Bill and Debbie Finch, from London, Ontario, worked. We filled in for them when they went on a three-week vacation. This was a more relaxed ministry, as we did not need to travel, and a student from Mexico studying at the Word of Life Bible Institute helped in the work. He and I met together each day for a teaching session.

The heat in Argentina became too much for me, so I visited the cardiologist. He told me, "Go home and lead a normal life. Running around the world is too hard on your heart." On the plane to Miami, I developed severe angina and felt as though I was having another heart attack. My medication didn't take the pain away. What do you do when you are 20,000 feet in the air and 20 minutes from Miami? I asked the stewardess to give me an aspirin and chewed it down. The pain went away.

Five paramedics swarmed into the plane when we landed; they took me through immigration and customs. From there, we went to a hospital ten minutes away. The doctors and nurses were from Cuba and spoke Spanish, so it was easy to communicate with them. I was kept there for two days for tests that all came back negative.

Because I nearly had another heart attack on the plane, Ruth and I decided our air travel was over. We would travel only where we could go by surface transportation. This meant the end of international ministry. We asked ourselves, "What is ahead? Will we be able to minister in the future?" I wasn't enthusiastic about settling down in a rocking chair. I discussed this with my pastor, Steven Mills. On July 1, 1997, I became the part-time associate pastor of church ministries at Central Baptist Church, in Brantford. Ruth and I are grateful to God, Steven Mills, and Central Baptist Church for giving us this ministry.

CHAPTER 20

Epilogue

The Greenslade Kids

Kathy was once asked, "What was it like growing up on the mission field?" Her answer was, "Normal." To our children, everything in this book was normal. At first, they thought life in North America was not normal, but now they all live successful lives in North America.

- **Tom** with his wife, Kathy, is the pastor of Prairie Baptist Church, near Noblesville, Indiana.
- **David** and his wife, Cindy, live in Los Angeles, California. He is an engineer with the Federal Express Company.
- **Kathy** had to return from her missionary service because of recurring, severe asthma. She teaches 5th grade at the North Toronto Christian Academy, in Toronto, Ontario.
- **Betty** serves with her associate pastor husband, Kevin Lewis, at Berean Bible Church, in Woodstock, Ontario.
- **Karen** and Grant Verdoold live in Sutton, Ontario. She types all the papers for her husband, who is completing his master of theology course at Heritage Seminary in Cambridge, Ontario.
- **Cindy** and her husband, David Middleton, live in Cambridge, Ontario. He is a firefighter with the Mississauga fire department.

All of our children serve God, for which we humbly praise Him. We also have 15 grandchildren, all of whom have accepted

Christ as Savior. Raising our children on the mission field has given us—and them—a rich heritage. They are now writing and sending us their memories. It makes fascinating reading for Ruth and me as we find out some things about them for the first time. I think they feel it is safe to do this now, as they are too old and too big for us to discipline.

On March 23, 2002, we became great-grandparents. Tom and Kathy's daughter, Jessica, gave birth to Jaxon Christopher Smith.

An Invitation for You

You have read in this book of evangelistic campaigns, of people being saved, of the changes for the better in lives, of social uplift in homes and communities. Wherever we went, our message was always the same: turn to Jesus Christ. He is accessible and ready to receive you, to forgive your sins and give you eternal life no matter how bad or good you are. In Matthew 11:28–29, Christ says, *"Come unto me all you who labor and are heavy laden, and I will give you rest. Take my yoke upon you and learn from me, for I am gentle and lowly in heart, and you will find rest for your souls."*

The message in Hebrews 4:15–16 states, *"For we do not have a High Priest who cannot sympathize with our weaknesses, but was in all points tempted as we are, yet without sin. Let us therefore come boldly to the throne of grace that we may obtain mercy and find grace to help in time of need."*

These verses show that the Lord Jesus understands and sympathizes with each one of us. Christ wants us to go boldly to Him with full confidence to receive mercy and grace in time of need. People worldwide have the need to have their sins forgiven and washed away. The apostle Paul states clearly in Ephesians 2:8–9, *"For by grace you are saved through faith, and that not of yourselves; it is the gift of God. Not of works, lest anyone should boast."*

Nothing we could ever do is good enough to merit eternal life. God, by His grace, gives it as a gift. He awaits you to receive that gift. I invite you to turn to Christ by faith, confess your sins, and ask Him to forgive you, and receive Him as Savior.

By doing this you will receive eternal life.

A Challenge for You

The apostle Paul states, *"Faith comes by hearing, and hearing by the word of God"* (Romans 10:17). People must turn by faith to Christ for eternal life and stop trusting in their good works. There is no other way. In order to do this, they need to hear the message of the Bible, the Word of God. The apostle Paul asks, *"How then shall they call on Him in whom they have not believed? And how shall they believe in Him of whom they have not heard? And how shall they hear without a preacher?"* (Romans 10:14).

There is an urgent need throughout the world for people to present the message of forgiveness of sins and the assurance of eternal life through Christ.

Have you seriously considered if God wants you to be one who carries this transforming message? You may feel as the prophet Jeremiah did, when he said, *"Ah, Lord God! Behold I cannot speak, for I am a youth"* (Jeremiah 1:6).

God wants you to look to Him, and not to yourself. God was with Jeremiah in all situations. When God calls a person to serve Him, He gives the confidence and the capacity to take His message anywhere and everywhere.

In Matthew 28:18–20 we read Christ's words, *"All authority has been given to Me in heaven and on earth. Go therefore and make disciples of all the nations, baptizing them in the name of the Father and the Son and the Holy Spirit, teaching them to observe all things that I have commanded you; and lo, I am with you always, even to the end of the age."*

Time and time again, in all our varied ministries, Ruth and I saw Christ's power and authority at work. He was always with us wherever we went. He watched over us and our children, and

186 FROM THE PRAIRIES TO PERU — AND BEYOND

He used us according to His eternal plan. He will do the same for you. Trust Him today, and follow Him wherever He may lead. By doing this, you will have the most fulfilling life possible.

The authors and the publisher of this book
invite you to correspond if you wish to know more
about Christ and the Christian life.

ABWE
P.O. Box 8585
Harrisburg, PA 17105-8585

For information regarding ABWE or books
by ABWE Publishing, visit our website:
www.abwe.org or phone toll free 1-877-959-2293.